# Old-fashioned and David Austin Roses

Barbara Lea Taylor

*Photographs by Juliet Nicholas*

**FIREFLY BOOKS**

## A FIREFLY BOOK

Published by Firefly Books Ltd. 2004

First published in 2004 in New Zealand by David Bateman Ltd.,
30 Tarndale Grove, Albany, Auckland, New Zealand

Copyright © 2004 Barbara Lea Taylor (text), Juliet Nicholas (photographs) & David Bateman Ltd

First Printing

**Publisher Cataloguing-in-Publication Data (U.S.)**

Taylor, Barbara Lea, 1929-
   Old-fashioned and David Austin Roses / Barbara Lea Taylor ; Juliet Nicholas, photographer. —1st ed.
[96] p. : col. photos. ;   cm.
Includes bibliographical references and index.
Summary: Introductory guide to growing old-fashioned and English roses, including hardiness zone information. Provides practical advice on how to plant, propagate, cultivate and landscape roses.
ISBN 1-55297-881-8
ISBN 1-55297-880-X  (pbk.)
1. Old roses. 2. English roses. I. Nicholas, Juliet, 1956- . II. Title.
635.9/33734 21      SB411.65.E53.T39  2004

**National Library of Canada Cataloguing in Publication**

Taylor, Barbara Lea
      Old-fashioned and David Austin roses / Barbara Lea Taylor ; photographs by Juliet Nicholas.
Includes bibliographical references and index.
ISBN 1-55297-881-8 (bound).--ISBN 1-55297-880-X (pbk.)
      1. Old roses. 2. English roses. 3. Rose culture. I. Nicholas, Juliet II. Title.
SB411.6.T39 2004          635.9'33734          C2003-905566-3

Published in the United States in 2004 by
Firefly Books (U.S.) Inc.
P.O. Box 1338, Ellicott Station
Buffalo, New York 14205

Published in Canada in 2004 by
Firefly Books Ltd.
3680 Victoria Park Avenue
Toronto, Ontario M2H 3K1

Printed in China through Colorcraft Ltd., HK

Page 1: Roses and companions in an exuberant perennial border.
Page 2: 'William Morris'
Title page: The Noisette rose 'Mme. Alfred Carrière'.

*For my mother, Meg Harwood, who could plant a cutting upside down and still make it grow, and my daughter, Marigold Southall, who has yet to get her hands dirty.*

## Acknowledgments

I would like to thank Marlea Graham of the Heritage Roses Group (U.S.A.) for her helpful advice, Juliet Nicholas for her professional skill and patience, and the nursery proprietors and gardeners who generously opened their gardens.

# Contents

Introduction    6

1. History    9

2. Once-flowering Old-fashioned Roses    13

3. Repeat-flowering Old-fashioned Roses    31

4. David Austin Roses    55

5. Cultivation    73

6. Landscaping with Old Roses    85

7. Decadent Diversions    90

Useful Addresses    92

Bibliography    94

Index    95

# Introduction

*What is a rose?*
*A cup of pure delight.*
ANON

This is my fourth book about roses. I have loved roses for more years than I am going to tell you. I still have so much to learn – and they are still so much fun.

When you are hooked by old-fashioned roses, it is the beginning of a love affair to last a lifetime – and there aren't too many of those around. They bring you not only fragrance and beauty, but fascinating tales from the past. When you plant a rose, you plant history with all its triumphs and disasters, trauma and trivia. They will give you far more than you expect or probably deserve and you will never, ever be bored.

Gardeners are practical people but most of us, whether or not we know it, are artists of a sort. Why else would we try year after year to paint pictures with plants on a constantly changing and often inhospitable canvas? Think of gardening as painting

with a very broad brush – and the really lovely thing about it is that if it doesn't work, we can rearrange it all next year. In spite of all our grumbling, we keep on trying because we love it, it's addictive and it keeps us off the streets.

There is no mystique about growing roses, old or new. It is easier than the books or the array of pest and disease control potions in garden centers would persuade us. There are roses to enhance every aspect of landscaping – riotous ramblers that fling themselves about, roses that climb sedately, shrub roses of substance, roses for hedges high or low, roses that are comfortable in beds, well-mannered roses for patios and pots, groundcover roses that scramble and trail.

There are roses that will light up our gardens three seasons out of four with foliage flowers and hips, and roses that will throw their hearts into just one exuberant flowering a year, but it will be so generous, so gorgeous, so overpoweringly lovely that we will not forget it.

In this book I have written about some of the old-fashioned roses and English roses I know well. I have placed them in basic groups – purists would divide them further – and I have listed a few roses that are not quite old enough to qualify but are too beautiful to leave out. There are many more roses I would have loved to include but I must leave them for you to discover.

Make room for roses. They may mortify the flesh a little but they will definitely lift your spirits like no other flower.

Left: Bourbon rose 'Zephirine Drouhin'

## Hardiness Zone Map

This map has been prepared to agree with a system of plant hardiness zones that have been accepted as an international standard and range from 1 to 11. It shows the minimum winter temperatures that can be expected on average in different regions.

Where a zone number has been given at the end of an entry, the number corresponds with a zone shown here. That number indicates the coldest areas in which the particular plant is likely to survive through an average winter. Note that these are not necessarily the areas in which it will grow best.

Because the zone number refers to the minimum temperatures, a plant given zone 7, for example, will obviously grow perfectly well in zone 8, but not in zone 6. Plants grown in a zone considerably higher than the zone with the minimum winter temperature in which they will survive might well grow but they are likely to behave differently. Note also that some readers may find the numbers a little conservative; we felt it best to err on the side of caution.

While the majority of roses will tolerate zone 4, roses grown in zones 4 and 5 will always require a degree of winter protection. For further information see page 78, Protection from cold.

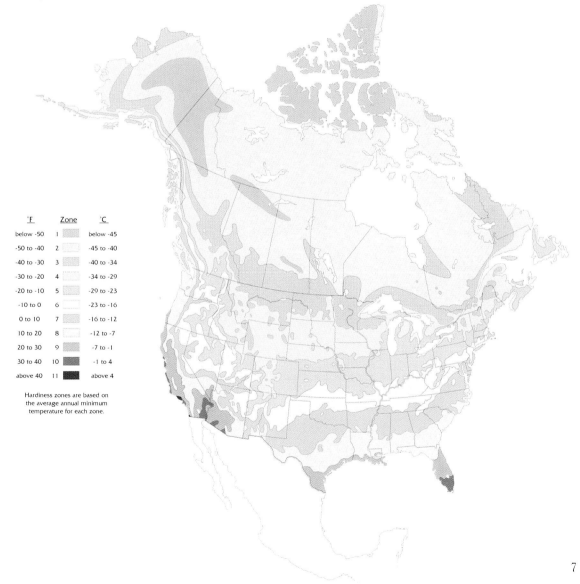

| °F | Zone | °C |
|---|---|---|
| below -50 | 1 | below -45 |
| -50 to -40 | 2 | -45 to -40 |
| -40 to -30 | 3 | -40 to -34 |
| -30 to -20 | 4 | -34 to -29 |
| -20 to -10 | 5 | -29 to -23 |
| -10 to 0 | 6 | -23 to -16 |
| 0 to 10 | 7 | -16 to -12 |
| 10 to 20 | 8 | -12 to -7 |
| 20 to 30 | 9 | -7 to -1 |
| 30 to 40 | 10 | -1 to 4 |
| above 40 | 11 | above 4 |

Hardiness zones are based on the average annual minimum temperature for each zone.

# CHAPTER 1

# *History*

*The rose and thorn,
the treasure and the dragon;
joy and sorrow
all mingled into one.*
THE PERSIAN POET, SADI, IN GULISTAN (ROSE GARDEN)

The history of the rose is interwoven with the history of humankind. Through the ages, medicine, religion, art and romance have all paid homage to the rose. We know that the rose is exceedingly ancient – older than humans and recorded time. Rose fossils believed to be at least 35 million years old have been found in Europe, Asia and North America. These prehistoric flowers had five petals and were not unlike *Rosa eglanteria* (syn *R. rubiginosa*), the Sweetbriar that grows wild in many parts of the world and we presume that early humans used them for food and possibly medicine.

It requires a great leap from the misty beginnings of time as we know it to reach the relative coziness of the ancient civilizations that have documented their love of the rose.

The first garden roses were probably grown in the Middle East and were carried along trade routes to spread over Europe.

The earliest significant depiction of the rose in history is a painting of what seems to be a single flowering rose on a fragment of fresco found during the excavation of the ruins of a Minoan palace built around 1700 BC on the island of Crete.

Oil of roses is mentioned by the Greek poets Homer in the 9th century BC and Sappho in the 6th century BC when she composed *Ode to the Rose* and

Opposite: 'Crown Princess Margareta'

'Comte de Champagne'

called it the queen of flowers. The island of Rhodes (which means roses) issued coins featuring a rose around 400 BC.

Roses have been cultivated in China for thousands of years. Confucius (551–459 BC) recorded that a large number of roses had been planted in the Imperial Gardens at Peking, and although it never seems to have been as popular as the peony and chrysanthemum, the rose was widely grown and represented in art.

Ancient Rome reveled in roses. Although they were cultivated extensively around Rome, there were not enough to satisfy the demand. Shiploads were imported from Egypt and kept fresh in copper containers during the journey, causing comments by the critics of the time that it might be more useful to fill the ships with much-needed grain.

Roses were used for table and house decorations, and Roman nobles carpeted the floors of their banqueting halls with petals. Servants showered the fragrant petals upon guests so generously that the occasional sleepy and drunken guest is said to have suffocated. It was believed that the perfume canceled the effects of the wine and was also an aphrodisiac. I doubt there is any truth in the former but I'm not sure about the latter. Wine and roses are a tried and true recipe for romance. When Cleopatra entertained she had her servants cover her bed as well as her floors with fresh rose petals.

It was the Romans who pre-empted the Victorian custom of planting a white rose on the grave of a young woman to symbolize purity and a red rose on the grave of a dead lover. Roses were used for medicinal purposes too and it is likely that Roman doctors accompanying soldiers carried rose seeds with them when they invaded Britain.

Roses and religion are intertwined. Monastery gardens have always included roses. The red rose is associated with the blood of Christ and the five petals of wild red roses are said to represent his five wounds. Rose windows decorate many cathedrals and churches; rosaries were originally made from dried rose hips – and sometimes still are.

In Jerusalem in 1187, the sultan Saladin used 500 camel-loads of rosewater to purify the mosque of Omar after the expulsion of the Crusaders.

Throughout the Middle Ages and Renaissance, the rose was prominent in the art, poetry, symbolism and heraldry of the Western world. In England, John Gerard's *Herball* published in 1633 described 18 roses in cultivation, some with illustrations.

When Carl Linnaeus published his landmark *Species Plantarum* in 1753, he listed 12 species of roses, giving them the Latin names we use today.

The importation of roses from China towards the end of the 18th century was a dramatic development

## Old-fashioned rose forms

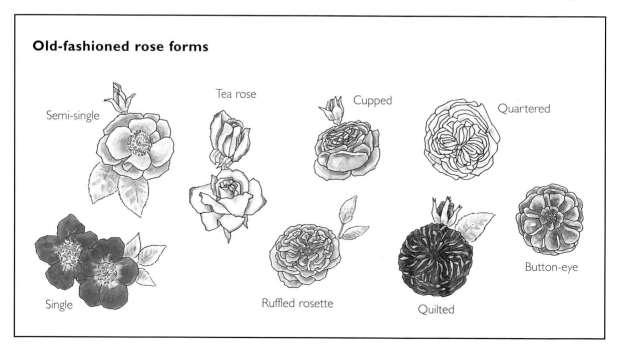

Semi-single

Tea rose

Cupped

Quartered

Single

Ruffled rosette

Quilted

Button-eye

in rose history; until that time most roses flowered only once in a season. China roses brought with them the gene that would endow future roses with remontancy – the ability to repeat flower.

The history of roses without the Empress Josephine would be like the history of Europe without Napoleon. Roses were her favorite flower. After her divorce from Napoleon, she retired to Malmaison, her estate outside Paris, where she employed the best botanists and hybridizers to create the most perfect roses – and the artist, Redouté, to immortalize them. Because of Josephine, rose seeds and sometimes the botanists themselves were given safe passage between England and France all through the Napoleonic wars. French hybridizers flourished under her patronage and 19th century France became the leading exporter of roses in the Western world.

In the 19th century, the increasing number of people spreading into suburbs and cultivating flower gardens created a new and lucrative market for rose breeders and nurserymen. Rose shows became popular events and there was much competition to produce the biggest and best rose. In England the Royal National Rose Society was formed with the Rev. S. Reynolds Hole as its president. In 1869 he published *A Book About Roses* which quickly became a best seller and is still regarded as a classic. In America in 1892, Henry B. Ellwanger published another classic, *The Rose*, an invaluable guide for rosarians of the day. Since then, such is the fascination of the rose, whole libraries of rose books have been written, but a rose we grow today is not all that much different from a rose someone grew and loved more than two thousand years ago and the principles of growing good roses have remained much the same through the ages.

Top right: Hybrid musk 'Penelope'
Bottom right: 'Mme. Lauriol de Barny'

CHAPTER 2

# Once-flowering Old-fashioned Roses

*A thing of beauty is a joy forever:*
*Its loveliness increases; it will never*
*Pass into nothingness; but still will keep*
*A bower quiet for us, and a sleep*
*Full of sweet dreams and health*
*And quiet breathing.*
JOHN KEATS, 'ENDYMION'

With a few exceptions, species roses and old European roses, as well as most ramblers, flower only once a year, usually in spring and early summer. Don't be deterred by this. A plant that has only one chance to perpetuate its kind puts all its energy into one, extravagant, heart-stopping fling. A rose that blooms from spring to winter doesn't need to be so profligate – and you will have to look after it longer and better! You might prefer a plant that flaunts its glory for a few wonderful weeks to one that thrusts forth flush after flush of production line perfection. Think of lilacs and daffodils in all their glory!

There are gorgeous roses in these groups, from simple singles to sumptuous full-petaled beauties, from compact bushes to rampageous ramblers, and you may find they fit your landscaping plans perfectly. Because once-flowering roses flower on the previous season's wood, any pruning should be done in summer as soon as possible after flowering has finished – unless, of course, you look forward to fall hips. For pruning advice, see the chapter on Cultivation, page 73.

Opposite: Gallica rose 'Complicata' frames a quiet corner.

## Species and near hybrids

These are the ancient wild roses of Asia, Europe and North America that date from the beginnings of rose history and from which all later hybrids evolved. Originally they would have been all five-petaled singles and many still are. Botanically, they can be divided into several sub-groups, but for practical reasons they are listed together here.

They can climb, hug the ground or make substantial shrubs but all of them are exceptionally hardy and, apart from watering until they become established and occasionally in hot dry summers, they need a minimum of care. Pests and diseases rarely attack them which means there is no need to spray. You can prune them annually or just now and then when they become too large. Most cope well with shady spots. Often, but by no means always, the flowers are insignificant, but interesting foliage and decorative hips are sufficient compensation. These are the perfect roses for the wild garden, the shrubbery – and for the gardener who finds a quiet pleasure in simplicity.

The Banksia roses were named for Lady Banks, wife of the eminent botanist Sir Joseph Banks who

sailed with James Cook around New Zealand and gave his name to Banks Peninsula. Later in life, he did much of the planning for Kew Gardens in London and dispatched a Scottish gardener, William Kerr, on a plant-hunting expedition to China. Kerr bought plants from the famous Fa Tee nursery and shipped them back to England. One of the few to survive the journey was *R. banksiae alba plena* ('White Banksia' or 'Lady Banks' Rose'), 1807.

Vigorous and thorn-free, this evergreen climber has draped many a veranda and covered many a barn with its shiny leaves and lavish clusters of small white double flowers smelling of violets. ZONES 4–10

### R. banksiae lutea
(Yellow Banksia), 1825
Imported from the same Chinese nursery, this rose has the same exuberant growth habits as *R. banksiae alba plena*. Masses of cascading clusters of fluffy, double, butter-yellow flowers are a sight to see in early spring when yellow is the bright wake-up call we need. Don't let its rampant habits trouble you. Because it has no thorns, it is easily controlled. ZONES 4–10

Above: *R. brunonii*
Below: *R. banksiae lutea*

### R. brunonii
(Himalayan Musk Rose), c.1823
A huge scrambling climber covered with fragrant clusters of single, creamy white, tissue-paper flowers prettily displayed among plentiful, long, gray-green leaves in summer. Bunches of red hips change from red to brown when the flowers have gone. Often confused with *R. moschata*, the original Musk rose. *R. brunonii* 'La Mortola' is a particularly fine garden form. ZONES 3–10

### R. dupontii
(thought to be a cross between *R. gallica* and *R. moschata*), pre-1817
Soft gray-green leaves on graceful arching branches, exquisite single blooms, then masses of little lipstick-

red hips in fall make this an endearing rose. Big, perfectly symmetrical blooms are milk-white with the faintest of blushes at the edge of petals and a coronet of golden stamens in the center. Flowers appear late in spring and continue through early summer. Give it plenty of room and grow this charmer as a big shrub or a climber. A lovely rose to grow beside water. Mine leans into an apple tree. Pick big branches or sprays for a vase. ZONES 4–11

### R. eglanteria

(syn *R. rubiginosa*, Sweet Briar), c.1594
A tall prickly shrub with arching canes and dark green leaves with a delicious apple fragrance after rain or when crushed – which isn't surprising when you consider roses and apples belong to the same family. Flowers are simple, pale pink singles in summer.

Shakespeare wrote about this sweet wild rose but may not have known that the leaves, not the flowers, are scented. In some areas it has spread so widely it is classed as a weed – but it's a pretty sight in the wild garden. Just prune it severely to keep it in check. ZONES 4–10

### R. foetida bicolor

(Austrian Copper), 1596
Big, single, poppy-like flowers are a dazzling orange-

Top left: *R. dupontii*
Top right: The rose hips of *R. glauca*
Above: *R. eglanteria*

flame with yellow stamens and a dark eye. It sometimes reverts to its yellow parent, *R. foetida*, and you get deep yellow and flame flowers on the same bush which is prickly and grows to about 6.5 x 6.5 ft. (2 x 2 m). This is a showstopper to light up your garden. A double yellow form, *R. foetida persiana*, was used in the late 19th century to breed the first yellow

Top left: *R. laevigata*
Top right: *R. moyesii*
Above: *R. foetida bicolor*

and orange Hybrid Tea and transmitted to all of its progeny a tendency towards the dreaded black spot. ZONES 4–11

### R. glauca
pre-1820, but a much older rose
If you can grow only one species of rose, choose this. I suppose you have to say the small, single, mauve-pink flowers are insignificant, but that's not important. Grow it for the wine-purple new canes,

the sea-green leaves tinted purple and the bunches of red hips that slowly turn a burnished coppery black. Flower arrangers love this graceful arching shrub. A total joy in fall and they don't come much tougher. ZONES 4–10

### R. laevigata
(Cherokee Rose), 1759
This is the state flower of Georgia. There is a pretty story that Cherokee women garlanded their hair with the flowers and believed this rose was once a princess who was changed to a rose to save her from her enemies. It's not hard to believe this in early spring when the big, single, slightly cupped white blooms with a crown of golden stamens are elegantly displayed against dark green polished foliage. This is a superb vigorous climber to cover a wall or a substantial fence, or fling itself in graceful ribbons from a tree, but it is happiest in a warm sheltered position and may not flower in a cold climate. Although it appears to have been established in the south long before any Europeans arrived, it is thought to be a native of China. ZONES 4–10

### R. moyesii
c.1890
An angular thorny shrub, but the dark, glowing-red,

single flowers with very prominent golden stamens, followed by decorative bunches of orange flagon-shaped hips, make it a welcome show-off among its more reticent spring companions. Good modern shrubs bred from this rose include 'Geranium', a dazzling scarlet, and 'Sealing Wax' with big, pink, single flowers. ZONES 4–10

### R. mulliganii
(often wrongly labeled *R. longicuspis*), 1917
Immense clusters of single white flowers nestle among shiny leaves on this wonderful climber which is almost evergreen in temperate climates.

Bill Grant, noted rosarian and connoisseur of species, says that if there were only one rose he could take to a desert island, this would be it! Below a high deck surrounding his house in California, he has a single plant that fills the garden with perfume and he expects it to reach "80 feet in the round – and the large umbels of tiny red hips make excellent bouquets at Christmas." ZONES 4–11

### R. roxburghii plena
(Chestnut Rose), 1814
Even if you didn't recognize this as a rose, you would be inclined to grow it as a handsome shrub. It has fresh, green, ferny foliage, buff-colored bark that flakes, chestnut-burred hips and the most exquisite crêpe paper frills of flowers in early spring – pale pink on the outside, deepening in the center and big for a species. It is also as tough as old boots – I grow it cruelly on a gravel driveway. ZONES 4–11

## Gallicas
Linnaeus, the 18th-century Swedish naturalist responsible for classifying plant species under Latin names, came up with the name Gallica for this most ancient rose family because he assumed it originated in Roman Gaul or Gallica, the old name for France.

We know that a Gallica rose was cultivated and used as a religious emblem by the Medes and Persians more than a thousand years before the birth of Christ. Early Greeks and Romans grew it for medicinal purposes and valued it particularly because the petals held their perfume when dried. Fresh petals were used to make fragrant oil and were perfect for strewing – which was a good way to perfume rooms when plumbing was primitive.

Ancient Romans were obsessed with the Gallica and Damask – and probably Alba – roses of the day. They garlanded themselves and decorated their houses with roses and used them in food and wine. They scattered petals in their baths and on their beds and even stuffed mattresses and pillows with them. Guests dined knee-deep in roses at all the best imperial banquets. The emperor Nero spent prodigious sums on rose petals and a Roman noble, Heliogabalus, assured himself of a mention in rose literature forever when his servants threw so may petals over his banquet guests that several suffocated. Although semi-double and fully double roses were grown by the Romans, the original wild *R. gallica* appears to have been a low-growing rosy-purple single.

In the Middle Ages a fragrant semi-double variety was used so much for medicinal purposes that it became known as the official rose of the apothecaries – *R. gallica officinalis* or 'The Apothecary's Rose'. At Provins near Paris it became the mainstay of a thriving industry producing potions, perfumes, powders, oils, distilled waters, conserves, ointments and almost anything that could be made from rose petals. When Marie Antoinette stopped overnight at Provins on her way to marry the future Louis XVI, she slept on a mattress stuffed with rose petals.

More utilitarian properties attributed to *R. gallica officinalis* were the ability to ease headaches, to control vomiting, dysentery and fevers, to help heal wounds and to cleanse the liver.

The rose that began it all is still in the catalogs, but the Gallica hybrids we lose our hearts to today were mostly bred in France in the 19th century and are a very different and flamboyant bunch – frilled,

Top: 'Anaïs Ségalas'
Above: 'Belle de Crécy'

quilled, ruffled or quartered – and totally gorgeous. Colors range from palest blush to choleric crimson purple – or splashed and striped with a mixture of the lot. Habit of growth is typically upright, compact and bushy and leaves are inclined to be crinkled and pointed at the tip.

Plants are hardy and not usually bothered by diseases although some are inclined to mildew a bit in late summer. However, by then the blooms have finished; you can cut the plant back and it will grow fresh new leaves.

Because Gallicas on their own roots are inclined to form thickets, it is best to buy budded plants. Make sure the bud-union is slightly above ground when planting and check regularly for suckers – unless, of course, you have space for a thicket.

### Anaïs Ségalas
1837, fragrant
To me this is one of the most beautiful Gallicas – and that's saying something. Clusters of fragrant, flat and immaculately frilled flowers are cerise-purple, fading to rosy lilac and finally lilac-gray. Atypically, the bush is angular and tall and can be used as a small climber with support. I have seen it used to great effect on a metal obelisk painted electric blue.
ZONES 4–10

### Belle de Crécy
1836, few thorns
A relaxed slender bush for a Gallica but a profuse bloomer. Delicious, full, flat, cerise-purple flowers with a ruff of reflexing petals around a button eye turn slatey-violet as they age. Romantics say the rose is named after a famous mistress of Louis XV, Mme. de Pompadour, who lived at Crécy, a suburb of Paris – but more prosaically, so did the breeder of the rose.
ZONES 4–10

### Cardinal de Richelieu
1840, fragrant
Sorry – but it's purple prose for this rich and magnificent rose – the darkest of the Gallicas. Crimson and ecclesiastical purple velvet petals reflex into a many-petaled ball that ages to slatey-lilac with a flick of pale reflexing petals in the center. The medium-sized shrub, with surprisingly smooth leaves and few thorns, flowers generously and appreciates regular pruning. A suitable rose to commemorate

Cardinal de Richelieu, the power behind the throne of Louis XIII. ZONES 4–9

### Charles de Mills
origin unknown, pre-1800
Introduced by the great French rose garden, Roseriae de l'Hay, there is no doubt this is one of the most spectacular of all old roses. No one knows just how old it is or to whom its name refers, or even if it's the correct name – I'm told the original label was smudged. But you can bet your boots he must have been dashing. Each time I see it, I am astonished and enchanted anew. The blooms are huge without being blatant, and beautifully formed – flat, many-petaled, quilled and quartered. The colors defy adequate description but rosarians do keep on trying. The best I can come up with is wine-red and plum-purple paling to magenta and lilac, then slatey-lavender before the petals fall. The bush is well foliaged with very few thorns. This is a rose that thickets readily if you don't remove suckers, but what could be nicer than a thicket of 'Charles de Mills'? A tough plant that can survive temperatures of -30°F (-34°C). ZONES 4–9

### Complicata
origin unknown
I've never quite worked out why this outstanding big shrub should be classed as a Gallica. Big, clear, rose-pink flowers with pale centers are borne on arching branches that will easily reach into trees. Mine reaches into the branches of an olive tree and together they cope beautifully with poor soil and very little care. Bright hips in the fall are an added pleasure. A rewarding rose that belies its name, which refers to the way the petals are folded together in the buds. ZONES 5–9

### Duchesse de Montebello
1829
What could be prettier than a compact, tallish, pear-shaped bush covered with identical, perfectly

Top: 'Duchesse de Montebello'
Above: 'Hippolyte'

formed, pale pink chiffon roses that might have graced the neckline of a Victorian ball gown? Foliage is soft gray-green and flowers grow in long sprays – lovely for picking. Named for the beautiful wife of an officer in Napoleon's army. Napoleon had a habit of choosing wives for his officers, often with catastrophically unhappy results. ZONES 4–10

'Cardinal de Richelieu'

## Hippolyte

early 19th century, few thorns

Flowers are not large but similar to 'Cardinal de Richelieu' in color with many petaled, flat blooms reflexing into balls of cerise and violet with pale highlights in the center. Although this rose is reasonably compact and suitable for a small garden, its habit of growth, with long arching branches covered with flowers, gives it a uniquely elegant air. Very few thorns are a bonus. An endearing rose. ZONES 4–9

## Rosa Mundi

(*R. gallica versicolor*), very old

Dip a blush pink rose in berry juice, then shake it and this is what you get. A sport of *R. gallica officinalis* and identical except for the color, it's a deliciously pretty rose with a background of fresh green leaves on a compact bush. It flowers prolifically and a massed bed or a hedge of it is a sight to see in spring and early summer.

Legend has it that the rose is named after a 12th-century beauty, Rosamund de Clifford, mistress of King Henry II of England. Henry's wife, Eleanor of Aquitaine, a woman who dealt decisively with life's little problems, cornered Rosamund in the palace maze and gave her a choice of death by poison or a knife – which is not much of a choice when you come to think of it. After Rosamund's death, the grief-stricken Henry picked a pretty pink striped rose

'Rosa Mundi'

Above: 'Complicata'
Right: 'Mme. Hardy'

that grew in the hedgerows and ordered that it be named after "fair Rosamund." Her grave can be seen at Godstow Nunnery in Oxford, England.

Some say she didn't die but was banished to the nunnery and lived out her life there – a choice often made by noblewomen when life became too complicated. Another story says *rosa mundi* simply means rose of the world and the rose is so named because it grew so freely. As there appears to be no record of it until the 16th century, this seems nearer the truth. So there you are. Life is so prosaic. Let's take the legend. ZONES 4–10

## Damasks

Pink, pretty and wonderfully fragrant, romantic Damask roses have delighted our eyes, perfumed our houses and flavored our food since ancient times. Their antiquity is beyond doubt. On the island of Crete, a single, faded, pink rose on a fresco painted by Minoan artists more than four thousand years ago has been identified as a form of Damask. Dried garlands of Damasks have been found in Egyptian tombs.

Cleopatra is said to have instructed her servants to soak the sails of her ship in Damask rose water before she sailed to meet Mark Anthony. (Sure beats a dab of perfume behind the ears!) The Roman emperor, Nero, imported shiploads of rose petals from Egypt to strew on floors, tables and couches at his notorious orgies, partly because the roses smelled better than the wine and the drunken guests. And speaking of notoriety, the aging and ulcerated King Henry VIII of England padded his clothes with sachets of Damask rose petals and lavender to mask less pleasant odors. But please don't let that put you off. I'm simply trying to illustrate the powerful fragrance of Damasks.

The summer-flowering Damask is believed to be a natural hybrid between *R. gallica* and a wild species called *R. phoenica*. There is, however, a repeat-flowering strain, *R. damascena bifera*, listed variously as 'Fall Damask', 'Four Seasons Rose' or 'Rose à Quatre Saisons', which flowers profusely in spring and then repeats intermittently through to fall.

Damasks are often taller than Gallicas and more lax in growth. Graceful, soft, deeply veined green leaves are long but rounded and pointed. Often there are stout hooked thorns and a little green ruff around the flowers.

### *R. damascena bifera*

(Fall Damask, Four Seasons Rose, Rose à Quatre Saisons), ancient

I love this unsophisticated rose. The muddled semi-double flowers are clear soft pink. The crinkled, fresh green leaves are a delight as they emerge in spring. As the name implies, it is capable of repeating until winter. ZONES 4–10

'Ispahan'

'Leda'

### Duc de Cambridge
fragrant

The largest and darkest of the Damasks with big, beautifully quilled flowers of deep rose-tinted purple. The bush is sprawling and prickly and responds well to pruning. ZONES 4–10

### Ispahan
(Pompon des Princes), pre-1832, fragrant

A superb rose with warm pink blooms opening flat and reflexing to show a ruff of incurving petals around a button eye. Makes a sizable bush with graceful arching branches and blooms for a very long time. ZONES 4–9

### Leda
(Painted Damask), 1827, fragrant

There is no mistaking this rose. Fat mahogany colored buds that look as if they have been chewed, open to layers of frilly milk-white petals brushed on the edges with carmine, as if touched by a paint brush. The usual good Damask foliage. ZONES 4–10

### Mme. Hardy
1832, very fragrant

I've heard Madame described as "all white lace and emeralds" by one of her many admirers, who considers her to be the most beautiful, summer-flowering white rose in the world. Slightly cupped blooms open flat and quartered, with a ring of petals folded in towards a jade green eye. Dark green foliage is the perfect backdrop.

Monsieur Alexander Hardy, rose breeder and director of the Luxembourg Gardens in Paris, named this rose for his wife who was Félicité Parmentier before her marriage. You will find her listed in the Albas. ZONES 4–10

## Albas

*Alba* is the Latin word for white, the color of all the early Alba roses, and the family dates back at least to ancient Rome. The Roman historian, Pliny, writing about gardening at the end of the 1st century AD, suggests the name might have been given because white roses grew wild in the British Isles which were known in ancient times as the Isles of Albion. Perhaps early Roman traders brought them there or perhaps they flourished in the hedgerows long before Roman ships touched the shores.

We know that Albas were widely grown throughout Europe during the Middle Ages and that artists of the Renaissance loved to paint them. The white flowers in Botticelli's *Birth of Venus* have been identified as Alba roses.

The original *Rosa alba* is thought to have been a natural hybrid of *R. damascena* (the 'Damask Rose') and a thornless, pure white form of *R. canina* (the 'Dog Rose'). Over time, pink hybrids have been introduced without any loss of the graceful form and delectable perfume. The delicacy and refinement of the flowers are in sharp contrast to the toughness of the plants which tend to be tall, strong, long-lived, exceptionally disease-resistant and cold hardy. They cope well with poor soil and can stand more shade than most. Often they can be recognized by their gray-green foliage.

Two of the oldest (pre-1600) are Alba Maxima ('Great Double White', 'Cheshire Rose', 'Jacobite Rose') and Alba Semi-plena ('White Rose of York'). Both these elegant roses can waft their fragrance over the entire garden. Semi-plena is one of the roses grown for the extraction of perfume at Kazanlik in Bulgaria. I had a hedge of this rose once and it perfumed the whole of the street where I lived. The big symmetrical blooms of Semi-plena are semi-single and milk-white with prominent golden stamens, and you get masses of bright little hips in fall. Maxima has big, luscious, creamy white double blooms. Bushes are tall and upright – approx 8 ft. (2.5 m) and foliage is pale gray-green. Lovely for hedges. ZONES 3–9

## Félicité Parmentier
1836, fragrant
Delectable, powder puff pink flowers full of swirling petals opening flat and reflexing are borne in clusters on a tall substantial bush. You can prune this rose to

Top: Alba Semi-plena ('White Rose of York')
Above: 'Königin von Dänemark'

suit your space, but it can grow to a big magnificent shrub in good soil – although it will tolerate poor soil. Félicité Parmentier, daughter of a French rose breeder, must have been quite something to have two roses named after her. She married Alexander Hardy, curator of the Luxembourg Garden in Paris who raised the exquisite white Damask that he christened 'Mme. Hardy'.

'Mme. Plantier'

I have been told by a descendant of the Hardy family that Félicité Parmentier, Mme. Legras de St. Germain and Mme. Plantier were sisters. It might be a nice idea to grow the French sisters together. They would do wonders for your early summer garden. ZONES 4–9

### Königin von Dänemark
(Queen of Denmark), 1826, very fragrant
A rose of exceptional beauty and fragrance in a family noted for both of these attributes. Blooms are warm pink, flat, perfectly quartered – and borne in such profusion that they weigh down the branches. A thorny shrub, shorter and bushier than most of the Albas, this is a truly queenly rose and extremely hardy. ZONES 4–10

### Mme. Legras de St. Germain
1846, fragrant, few thorns
Even the name reads like a poem. Madame is an aristocrat to her last petal and perhaps the most beautiful of the ivory white roses. Beautifully formed, slightly cup-shaped rosettes full of petals open flat to show a hint of lemon in the centers. Flowers bloom all along flexible arching branches which are almost thornless and can be encouraged to climb a little. Mme. Legras de St. Germain is reputed to have been a sister of Félicité Parmentier. ZONES 4–10

### Mme. Plantier
1835, few thorns
A little bit of mystery lies in the breeding of this rose which sometimes masquerades as a Damask, sometimes a Noisette. Pink-tinted buds open to full-petaled ivory flowers that turn milk-white and reflex to show a jade green eye. Long, relaxed, almost thornless canes will form a sprawling shrub or will climb if given the chance. Try it with a non-rampant purple or mauve-blue clematis and let it cascade from a tree. In the 19th century it was popular for brides' bouquets and also for planting in cemeteries as a memorial rose. ZONES 4–10

### Maiden's Blush
(Cuisse de Nymphe, La Royale, La Séduisante, Virginale, Incarnata), pre-16th century, very fragrant
A graceful, arching, shrub rose, known in France as 'Cuisse de Nymphe' ("Nymph's Thigh"), which is a perfect description of the delicate flesh pink color of its flowers. Victorian England couldn't cope with that sort of vulgarity (even the word *leg* was considered offensive if it was attached to a woman) and re-christened it rather prissily 'Maiden's Blush'. There are – or were – 'Great Maiden's Blush' and 'Small Maiden's Blush' depending on the size of the flowers, not the maiden. Blooms are loosely double, totally charming and smell divine. If you have a choice, go for 'Great Maiden'. ZONES 4–11

## Centifolias
For a long time, Centifolias were thought to be as ancient as Albas, Gallicas and Damasks but research has shown them more likely to be the result of a series of crosses by Dutch breeders which resulted in a distinct group appearing in the 16th century. This full and fragrant "rose of a hundred petals" or

Above: 'Village Maid'
Right: 'Fantin-Latour'

"*rosier de cent feuilles*" was so lovely that it became a favorite subject for the Dutch and Flemish flower painters of the day and later was immortalized in Redouté's *Les Roses*.

Packed with soft petals, Centifolias are not only beautiful but are considered to be the most heavily fragrant of all roses and are cultivated extensively in Provence for their perfume. In England, Centifolias became known as cabbage roses, which is a reasonably accurate though prosaic description – and I suppose we could compare its fat buds to brussel sprouts.

Typical habit of growth is lax and open; leaves are large and often attractively wrinkled and serrated. Flowers heavy with petals are inclined to hang down so it's a good idea to plant your Centifolia roses in a raised part of the garden where you can look up into the sumptuous and intricately wrapped heart of the rose. These roses are summer flowering, with a few exceptions, noted below.

'Tour de Malakoff'

### Centifolia Variegata
(Cottage Maid, Village Maid, La Rubanée, Belle des Jardins), 1845
I have listed the most common of the many names this delicious striped rose has inspired over the years. Big, blush-cream, cupped, double blooms are striped in magenta-lilac. The bush is vigorous and freely produces lovely long sprays of blooms ideal for flower arrangements. This rose is capable of repeating a little in a good year. ZONES 4–10

### Fantin-Latour
date and origin unknown
A mystery rose with a dash of China blood and no records of its past, this rose was named after the great 19th-century French painter, Henri Fantin-Latour, whose favorite flower was the rose. If you have ever flipped through a coffee table book of old roses, you

will have seen it – an exquisite ballerina of a rose. A hundred blush-pink petals twirl and frill into a big soft flat flower with a reflexing ruff around a button eye. It grows to a tall shrub if left unpruned. ZONES 4–9

### Petite de Hollande
(Pompon des Dames), c.1800
With a low-growing but bushy habit of growth, this is the ideal Centifolia for a small garden or a container. Stylish and charming rose-pink flowers are small but perfectly formed. ZONES 5–9

### Tour de Malakoff
1856, fragrant
This is a distinctive and magnificent, big, bold, loosely double rose opening magenta and purple and aging to shades of violet. Sometimes it's called 'The Taffeta Rose' because the colors can merge with age and weather and become blurred and almost iridescent like old water-marked taffeta. Habit of growth is tall and sprawling which means the bush is better with support and can be encouraged to climb a little if you like. ZONES 4–10

## Mosses
Moss roses are very like Centifolias except they have a moss-like growth on stems and sepals which looks like a disease but in reality is very pretty. In fact, the Moss rose is thought to have begun as a mutation on a Centifolia rose but along the way other roses have contributed to its breeding. Moss can be soft and downy or stiff and whiskery and is usually aromatic when touched. Some roses have a lot, some have very little, but this charming packaging adds another dimension to a beautiful rose and it would be hard not to be enchanted by a pink and perfumed Moss rose in its ferny bed.

After enjoying a burst of sentimental popularity in the 19th century, Mosses went out of fashion and their number dwindled in the catalogs. However, rumor has it they are back in style – maybe even trendy. Perish the thought. One of the reasons could be that some of them, perhaps due to a splash of China blood, are capable of repeating – or maybe we just need something soft and pretty apart from the computer.

Habit of growth is inclined to be more upright than the Centifolias, but the heavenly fragrance is the same. Mosses are summer flowering, with a few exceptions, noted below.

### Comtesse de Murinais
1843
A delicious, faintly blushing, white moss, opening flat with a little ruff of reflexing petals in the center. Long flared sepals enclosing pink-tinged buds are covered with powerfully aromatic moss. Luxuriant crinkly dark green foliage on a tall bush, better with support. ZONES 5–9

### Crested Moss
(Chapeau de Napôléon, Cristata), 1826
Heavily mossed and fringed sepals project from the buds in such a way that they resemble little three-cornered hats like the French *tricorne* that Napoleon wore.

Deep pink flowers are Centifolia-like, scented and pretty on a hardy, healthy bush. ZONES 4–9

### Henri Martin
1863, few thorns, fragrant
Big claret-red flowers are loosely double and borne in profuse clusters on a wide spreading bush with excellent foliage. Not much moss but spectacular in full bloom and tough as old boots. ZONES 4–9

### Mme. Louis Levêque
1874, fragrant
Not a lot of moss but the flowers are sheer perfection

'Henri Martin'

27

Above: 'William Lobb'
Left: 'Mme. Louis Levêque'

and instantly recognizable. Silky crumpled petals roll back in semi-circles in very large, cupped blooms just the right shade of silvery pink with creamy undertones. My bush is tall, upright, a bit ungainly, better with support – and I love it to pieces. Treat it well and it will repeat bloom in the fall. ZONES 4–10

### William Lobb

(Old Velvet Moss, Duchesse d'Istrie), 1855, fragrant

My second-favorite moss rose. Moss-covered crimson buds open to lilac-purple petals that curl and swirl into a loosely double flower. As the flower opens, you see golden stamens and a flick of white. It's a tall shrub or small climber – lovely against a dark green trellis. ZONES 5–10

## Ramblers

Put briefly, climbers are bred to grow upwards, are inclined to be stiff and often bare at the base; ramblers have more pliant canes, will ramble in all directions and produce new growth from the base. Ramblers can be trained up, over or along. In spring and early summer they do a magnificent job of covering fences, pergolas, summerhouses, banks, tree-stumps, outhouses, dwelling houses – almost anything that could be improved with a flowery coverlet. For a truly spectacular effect, grow them up trees and let them trail. Most flower only once but some are evergreen in temperate climates which means you get year-round leafy cover. Most have a pleasant rather than a heavy fragrance.

*R. banksiae*, a magnificent evergreen rambler, is listed under species. A few ramblers are listed under repeat-flowering roses.

### Adelaide d'Orléans

1826, partly evergreen

Clusters of bright pink little buds open to flat, pink-tinted, creamy ruffles of flowers that will trail from arches, pergolas and trees like weeping Japanese cherry blossoms. This is a very pretty and graceful rambler with evergreen foliage in temperate climates. Said to smell of primroses, although it doesn't to me, this rose was bred by Antoine Jacques, head gardener at Château de Neuilly, the home of Louis Philippe, Duc d'Orléans and named for one of his three daughters. Two years later, Jacques introduced 'Félicité-Perpétue', also with creamy pink, full-petaled pompons of flowers and the hardiest rambler I know. The story goes that Jacques and his wife planned to name a rose after the next baby if it was a girl. Twin girls were born and christened Félicité and Perpétue, commemorating Christian martyrs of 203 AD. Interestingly, Félicité-Perpétue is capable of repeating. ZONES 4–9

## Albéric Barbier
1900, evergreen, copes with shade

In my book, this is the greatest rambler of all time – a rampantly healthy, shiny-leafed rambler (evergreen in warm regions) you can grow as a country hedge or keep to city limits. If you can resist picking them, elegant lemon-yellow buds open to big, muddled, double creamy blooms, often with buttery centers. Buds and flowers are beautifully framed by dark green leaves. It makes a perfect hedge because the vigorous pliable canes are easy to train sideways along a fence.

Near my back door, I have a courtyard enclosed on three sides by a high wall of 'Albéric Barbier', but you can keep it smaller if you wish. I've seen it used as a pillar rose and a weeping standard. It does repeat a little – which is a surprise and a joy – but you get only one real flush of bloom. ZONES 4–10

## American Pillar
1902

Big, single, vivid pink flowers with pale centers are borne in clusters. Vigorous, thorny and suckering, it will cover any structure with a cheerful splash of color – spectacular in full summer bloom. Leaves are luxuriant and glossy but prone to mildew. The rose can cope with this if you don't mind the look of the mildew. Plant it if you want to create a mid-summer spectacle but be warned – with its vigor and thorns it is not a "cosy" rose. ZONES 5–10

Top: 'American Pillar'
Above: 'Albéric Barbier'

'Gardenia'

a long time and looks superb covering pergolas or falling from trees. It copes well with a certain amount of shade. The name refers to the appearance, not the perfume. ZONES 7–10

### Laure Davoust
1834
Pompons of lilac-pink blooms, often with a green eye, are tightly packed into immense clusters. You wouldn't find a prettier sight than an arbor or veranda fringed with this Victorian charmer. It's a vigorous grower but pliable canes are easily trained and there are very few thorns. It is spectacular as a weeping standard. ZONES 4–10

### Veilchenblau
(Violet Blue, Blue Rambler), 1909
Thankfully, not a blue rose, but clusters of small double flowers ranging in color from deepest violet through rosy-lilac to lavender-gray, with yellow stamens and a flick of white highlight. This vigorous, healthy rambler is a memorable sight in full bloom in spring and early summer. Train it horizontally against a wall and underplant it with fuchsias in complementary colors. ZONES 5–9

'François Juranville'

### François Juranville
1906, few thorns
Often confused with the more common Albertine, but this rose is more beautiful. Flowers open flat and double, sometimes quilled, in a mix of pinks – primarily coral – lit by yellow at the base of the petals. Graceful growth and one long spectacular summer blooming. ZONES 4–10

### Gardenia
1899
Long, pointed, pale primrose buds open to full, muddled, double flowers of ivory-white with a touch of primrose in the centers. Dark glossy leaves frame the pale flowers beautifully. 'Gardenia' is a vigorous healthy plant that, given a warm spot, blooms for

CHAPTER 3

# Repeat-flowering Old-fashioned Roses

The importation of roses from China towards the end of the 18th century was a dramatic and far-reaching development in the history of the rose. When China roses reached the Western world they brought with them the gene that would enable future roses to repeat flower. They effectively revolutionized the garden appeal of the rose, endowing it with a long flowering period and new forms and colors.

## China roses

Foreigners were forbidden to enter China until 1842 but as every gardener who carries pruning shears (secateurs) in the glove compartment will know, plant hunters are a fearless and devious band. It follows that seeds, cuttings and plants were collected from China much earlier than that.

In the late 1700s, a pink form of *R. chinensis* reached England by way of the Netherlands and was first mentioned growing in the garden of a Mr. Parsons. Named 'Parsons' Pink China' at the time, it is now known as 'Old Blush' and is still one of the most appealing roses we grow. At about the same time, a rich, bright crimson rose was imported, via the Calcutta Botanic Gardens (a handy resting place for roses en route from China), by English nurseryman Gilbert Slater and christened 'Slater's Crimson China'.

These roses, together with the pink 'Hume's Blush' imported from a Chinese nursery in 1810 and 'Park's Yellow', collected by a Royal Horticultural

Right: 'Cécile Brunner'

Above: 'Mutabilis'
Left: 'Gruss an Teplitz'

Society member in 1824, are the stud roses responsible for the ability to repeat flower in later roses.

We still grow a few of the early Chinas, as well as their more recent hybrids. They flower continuously or in repeated flushes, come in a variety of forms, their habit of growth is usually open and twiggy and to grow them is to love them.

### Cécile Brunner
(Sweetheart Rose), 1894, climber
Renowned for its exquisitely formed little buds (perfect for a vase) and sprays of porcelain pink flowers, this rose is available as a bush or climber. I recommend the vigorous, fast-growing climber. Plant it to cover a warm wall or leave it unsupported to form a huge cascading flowery bush – spectacular near a

pond. I've seen it used as a hedge kept to a moderate size with hedge-clippers.

Our grandmothers and great-grandmothers loved this rose and called it 'Cecil' rather than 'Cécile', which is odd because it was named after a daughter of the Swiss breeder. ZONES 4–9

## Comtesse du Cayla
1902

Immensely stylish but never brash, the 'Comtesse' is sure to be noticed in your garden. Loose, nodding, semi-double blooms are brilliant flame and copper with a flick of gold and a sweet pea fragrance. Glossy foliage is tinged with bronze. Although classed as low growing and compact, my bush was planted beside 'Souvenir de Mme. Léonie Viennot' and has managed to climb up through her branches to create a gorgeous combination of blooms. Try it – but in a warm sunny spot. The rose is named for Zoë Talon, the wise and witty last mistress of Louis XVIII. ZONES 7–11

## Gruss an Teplitz
(Virginia R. Coxe), 1897, very fragrant

You will smell the heavenly perfume of this red rose before you see it. Clusters of informal double flowers are velvety crimson with blue overtones and a silvery sheen on the reverse of the petals. Young foliage is bronzy-purple. You can prune to keep it as a shrub or grow it as a moderate climber. Try it as a hedge against a white picket fence. Like many red roses, it's prone to mildew late in the season but it can cope if you can. ZONES 5–9

## Mutabilis
(Tipo Ideale), introduced 1932 but much older – perhaps it grew in a mandarin's garden?

An astonishing rose with a charm all its own. If you think a simple single rose would bore you, plant 'Mutabilis' and you will feel like the Queen in *Alice in Wonderland* who could believe six impossible things before breakfast. From delicate pointed

'Old Blush'

buds, masses of big, butterfly, single flowers open primrose and honey, change to rosy-buff and finally to crimson before the five petals fall. Or they might do it in reverse – you can't be certain. The airy but shrubby bush flowers prolifically and will grow as big as you let it. Given warmth, food and support, it will climb. It makes a superb hedge in flower from spring through fall. This rose is the perfect bridge between pink and yellow roses in your garden. ZONES 5–10

## Old Blush
(Parson's Pink China, Old Pink Monthly), introduced late 1700s but much older

This important and indispensable ancient rose blooms in monthly flushes and will give you the first blooms of spring and the last blooms of fall. What's more, it is totally enchanting. Not an elegant single or a voluptuous double but something in between – a charming semi-double, rosy pink with a silvery reverse to the petals. Growth is airy and canes are slender and easily trained. Bush and climbing forms are available but I strongly recommend the climber. Grow it against a sunny wall – around a window perhaps. You will love that flowery bounty in early spring. ZONES 6–9

'Comte de Chambord'

'Jacques Cartier'

## Perle d'Or

(Yellow Cécile Brunner), 1883

Not flashy but a thoroughly likable, largely disease-free, dependable rose that just keeps on flowering from spring through to winter. Flowers are not yellow and not much like those of 'Cécile Brunner'. Big clusters of buds open to double blooms with distinctive narrow petals of soft apricot flushed with pale gold and shorter in the center. Twiggy canes that appear delicate belie the plant's toughness. Although classed as low growing, 'Perle d'Or' can reach at least 6 ft. (2 m) and even climb in warm climates. ZONES 4–9

## Portlands

These roses with a mixed ancestry of Damask, Gallica, Centifolia and China were introduced in England towards the end of the 18th century and named in honor of the Duchess of Portland. Long blooming, sturdy and compact, they were numerous and popular well into the 19th century and contributed to the breeding of later roses. A few of the best remain today and are excellent shrubs for smaller gardens or mass planting in beds. Looking like a shorter version of Damasks, the bushes are thickly foliaged and in spring the flowers are often borne "on the shoulder," which means they have short stems and nestle prettily into the foliage. Portland roses are remontant, i.e., they repeat flower from spring onwards. However, as is the case with most repeat-flowering old roses, how well they repeat flower, and whether the flowering continues into fall, depend on how well they are looked after (see the chapter on Cultivation, page 73).

## Comte de Chambord

1863, very fragrant

Bright pink buds open to big, fully double blooms opening flat with layers of petals, rich pink at the center, paling to a soft lilac. A beautiful rose that you would want on a hat. Bred by a New York rose grower, Daniel Boll, the rose was named after his wife and known as 'Mme. Boll'. However, the rose was not marketed in the U.S. but sent to France where it was given the name of a French nobleman. ZONES 5–9

## Jacques Cartier

(Marchesa/Marquise Boccella), 1842

A soft, clear pink rose that opens flat with layers of petals, often quartered with a ruff of incurving

'Rose de Rescht'

petals in the center and a button eye. The neat rounded bush is studded with flowers held up straight in ample foliage. Grow it with blue or purple perennials. Named for the French navigator who explored the Gulf of St. Lawrence, this hardy rose copes well with cold. If exhibited in the U.S., it must be labeled 'Marquesa Boccella'. ZONES 4–9

### Rose de Rescht
discovered in Iran in the 1930s, but a much older rose A brilliant jewel of a rose poetically described by Miss Nancy Lindsay who discovered it as "… a sturdy yard-high bush of lizard green, perpetually emblazoned with full camellia flowers of pigeons' blood, ruby irised with royal purple …," which says it all. However, unless pigeons have fuchsia-colored blood, it's a little off the mark. ZONES 5–9

## Noisettes
So many old roses could tell extraordinary stories – romantic and tragic – about the people concerned with their conception and introduction. That's part of their allure. Show me a rose and I'll tell you a story. But by the time it has reached me down the years, who can be sure of the facts?

The facts concerning the introduction of the first Noisette seem straightforward. In the early 1800s, John Champneys, a plantation owner in Charleston, South Carolina, bred a pretty pink climbing hybrid of 'Parson's Pink China' ('Old Blush') and *R. moschata* (the 'Musk Rose'). He called this rose 'Champneys' Pink Cluster'. He eventually gave plants to Philippe Noisette who had arrived in Charleston in the late 18th century and established a nursery. Noisette bred from it and raised a smaller but fuller-petaled rose he called simply 'Blush' (now known as 'Blush Noisette'). He sent it to his brother, a nurseryman in Paris, where it became hugely popular. French breeders introduced a yellow strain by crosses with 'Park's Yellow China'. Further hybridization with Tea roses produced a whole new group of climbers called Noisettes.

The development of Noisettes ran parallel to that of Bourbons and Teas and added a new color – a soft yellow – to the predominant pinks and reds of climbing roses of the day.

Not that all Noisettes are yellow. They can be milk-white, old ivory, apricot mousse or tea-washed pink, but a sheeny, silky yellow is their trademark. All of them are extremely beautiful and many are powerfully fragrant. Noisettes thrive in a sunny, warm situation. Although some can be grown successfully in zone 6, they are not cold hardy roses and will need winter protection to survive in this climate zone. Most will give you big displays in spring and fall with repeat blooms through summer.

### Alister Stella Gray
(Golden Rambler), 1894, few thorns
Very double blooms that open flat are pale yellow on the outer edges, amber in the centers. This is a big sprawling bush, cascading hundreds of blooms; it will stop you in your tracks. Grow it to lean over a gazebo or summerhouse or simply as a big spectacular shrub. Although vigorous, the thin canes are easily controlled. Alister Stella Gray was the son of an English rose breeder whose wife died

Top: 'Crépuscule' tumbling gracefully over a wall.
Above: 'Alister Stella Gray'

when Alister was born – hence the unusual middle name. ZONES 7–10

### Céline Forestier

1842, fragrant

Pointed buds striped ivory and cerise, open to big, flat and quartered, butter-yellow and clotted cream flowers. It begins with a magnificent spring flowering and repeats into fall. A robust and healthy climber – give it a warm wall and you will be well rewarded. ZONES 7–10

### Crépuscule

1904, few thorns

If you have space for only one apricot rose, choose this one. Masses of loosely double blooms open deep apricot and pale to a soft twilight glow as they age. A big, gracefully arching shrub or controllable climber with glossy disease-resistant foliage, the rose is perfectly named. *Crépuscule* means twilight. Spectacular in early summer when it is a mass of blooms from top to bottom, it repeats well until winter. Grow it with purple irises, pansies and clematis. Wonderful over an arch or as a superb hedge. ZONES 7–11

### Jaune Desprez

(Desprez à Fleur Jaune), 1830, few thorns

Totally exquisite (I am sparing with that word!) double blooms shaded primrose, peach and pinky buff open flat, sometimes with muddled inner petals, sometimes quartered. It displays vigorous growth and can cope better with poor soil, shade and a colder climate than most Noisettes. Generous flowerings in spring and fall, repeats in between. Grow it on an old brick wall if you can find one. ZONES 6–10

### Lamarque

(Général Lamarque, The Maréchal), 1830, few thorns, fragrant

Clusters of big ruffles of milk-white petals with a hint of lemon in the center are borne in profligate abundance against a backdrop of healthy pale green

Above: 'Céline Forestier'
Right: 'Lamarque'

leaves. 'Lamarque' in full bloom is a sight to see. Ideal for a covering a long pergola walk, or any large structure in the garden that you want to look simply glorious. In a warm climate, it repeats in great flushes of bloom from spring to winter. ZONES 6–10

### Mme. Alfred Carrière
1879, few thorns, very fragrant
A rumpled organza skirt of milk-white petals with faintest blush gives this rose an ethereal quality that belies its toughness. Add a robust constitution, pliable canes that are easy to train, a long flowering period and a heady perfume, and you have the perfect "go anywhere" climber. A delightful rose to look up to on a pergola. Madame even copes well with shade and cold. ZONES 6–10

## Bourbons
Once upon a time, farmers on the French Isle de Bourbon (a small island off the coast of Madagascar, now known as Réunion) had the pretty habit of

dividing their fields with hedges of roses. A natural hybrid which was to become the first Bourbon rose occurred between 'Parson's Pink China' ('Old Blush') and *R. damascena bifera* ('Quatre Saisons', 'Fall Damask'). These two roses had little in common except the ability to flower perpetually, which they bequeathed to their offspring.

In 1817 a French botanist, M. Emile Bréon, who had been sent to establish a botanical garden on the island, sent seeds of this new hybrid to M. Antoine Jacques, head gardener to the Duke of Orléans (later to become King Louis Philippe), at the Château de Neuilly where it was later painted by Redouté. A second-generation rose was raised; French hybridizers took it from there and Bourbon roses became immensely popular.

Here was a rose that had it all – charm, style, vigor and a heavenly old-world fragrance inherited from its Damask parent. What's more, it could keep on flowering all through summer and still produce a generous flush of blooms in fall. If you like your roses lavish, these sumptuous full-petaled and versatile roses are for you. Many are inclined to climb but can be kept as bushes with support or pegged down in the old-fashioned manner. For continuity of flowers and good fall blooms, feed regularly.

### Blairii No. 2
1845
This rose has gorgeous, fat, full-petaled flowers opening flat, deep pink with the center paling at the edges. A totally beautiful plant that blooms its heart out in spring but, unlike most Bourbons, rarely repeats – at least for me. Strong thorny canes fling themselves about, so it's best grown as a climber – or a very big mounding shrub if you have the space. I've seen it grown with spring flowering clematis and that was a sight to see. ZONES 5–10

Top left: 'Blairii No. 2'
Left: 'Honorine de Brabant'

'Louise Odier'

'Mme. Isaac Pereire'

## Honorine de Brabant
date of introduction unknown
Full-petaled, cupped blooms are blush pink speckled and striped with lilac and deep rose pink. Long, lovely, pale green leaves are an inheritance from the Musk rose.

The bush is tall and robust. I like to grow it near 'Mme. Isaac Pereire'. The vivid color of this rose is both cooled and highlighted by 'Honorine de Brabant's' delicate stripes. ZONES 4–9

## Louise Odier
1851, fragrant
Big, double, camellia-like flowers are an unvarying warm pink with each petal precisely in place. The bush is robust and flowers prolifically. Flowers are held on long stems and last well in a vase. A thoroughly dependable rose. ZONES 4–10

## Mme. Isaac Pereire
1881, very fragrant
One of the most fragrant of all roses, with enormous, sumptuous, many-petaled blooms. The color is a jewel-like, rich rose with overtones of purple. You can't have everything and if the habit of growth is awkward and angular, the foliage a little sparse and, perish the thought, there could be a susceptibility to black spot, do we care? So much beauty is worth a little maintenance perhaps? Best trained on a pillar, trellis or against a wall and fed well.

Mme. Isaac Pereire was the wife of a Parisian banker during the reign of Napoleon III.

Was the rose named after her because she was beautiful, I wonder, or because her husband was rich enough to buy the name from the breeder? Perhaps both.

A pale pink sport of the rose, 'Mme. Ernst Calvat', introduced in 1889, is equally lovely in a gentler way and just as fragrant but with better foliage. New leaves are burnished bronze. Why not grow these roses together? ZONES 5–10

## Mme. Lauriol de Barny
1868, fragrant
I wouldn't be without this rose. Big double blooms, often quartered and frilled, are silvery rose-pink with lilac undertones – and sometimes an iridescent mix of these shades, like the water-marked sheen on

'Souvenir de la Malmaison'

'Souvenir de St Anne's'

silk taffeta. The perfume is slightly fruity – like a delectable wine. It can be grown as a big shrub but is better treated as a moderate climber and given support. ZONES 5–10

### Souvenir de la Malmaison
1843 bush, 1938 climber, very fragrant
This big, powder pink, fragrant and devastatingly beautiful rose remains high on the list of world favorites. Yes, I know the fat buds turn to liver pâté in wet weather but life wasn't meant to be easy – and otherwise, you can't fault it. Bush and climbing forms are available but you will get more pleasure from the climber. It's tough, vigorous, forgiving and extremely floriferous. Fall blooms are particularly lovely. Against conventional advice to protect the plant from rain under eaves (where a lack of sun and breeze could make the plant damp and miserable), I grow mine over a pergola where the blooms on top are open to wind and rain and are a constant flowery delight from upstairs windows. The name of the rose commemorates the Empress Josephine's garden at Malmaison, the estate outside Paris to which she retired after her divorce from Napoleon. ZONES 5–9

### Souvenir de St Anne's
1950, very fragrant
If you can't cope with mushy buds, plant this very elegant, comparatively modern sport of 'Souvenir de la Malmaison' discovered in a garden near Dublin. The soft, pale pink color and heavenly fragrance are the same but petals are fewer. A tall bushy shrub. ZONES 5–9

### Zephirine Drouhin
1868, thornless, fragrant
Frilly double blooms of unrelieved cerise pink are borne in profusion on this popular rose. Would it be as popular if it were thorny? As a big shrub or a small climber, it's a cheerful rose against a white wall and, because it's thornless, it's easily managed and ideal for planting near doorways and paths. It flowers generously but watch for mildew. 'Kathleen Harrop', a pale pink sport of this rose, is also thornless. Try them together as a hedge. ZONES 5–10

## Hybrid perpetuals
From Bourbons and a variety of other parents, a class of repeat-flowering roses referred to as Hybrid Perpetuals evolved. In the main they were big exhibition-type roses, the darlings of the rose shows so popular in the 19th century. New roses were hybridized at an astonishing rate with the emphasis on big spectacular flowers rather than hardiness and health. For a time there were thousands, but most

have disappeared. Two examples of superstars of the 19th century not often grown today are 'Général Jacqueminot' and 'Frau Karl Drushki'. 'General Jack', a shapely perfumed red rose grown under glass for florists, became so popular in New York that it was claimed "there is not a bosom in New York on which the General has not nestled." Although it has been superseded by better red roses, it has often played a part in their ancestry. 'Frau Karl Drushki', a big queenly rose, pink in the bud, opening pure white, was for a long time regarded as the best white rose available. Most Hybrid Perpetuals repeat flower from spring to fall.

## Ferdinand Pichard
1921
A big, stylish, striped confection of pink and magenta-purple petals curling within a cup, and one of the last Hybrid Perpetuals to be introduced commercially, this is a consistently popular rose. Habit of growth is upright and vigorous, but suitable for a small garden. Makes a spectacular hedge. ZONES 4–9

## Mrs. John Laing
1887, very fragrant, few thorns
The blooms are very double, shapely and silvery pink. I love the way the inner petals curl around its cabbagey heart while outer petals provide a frame. A healthy plant that flowers profusely, it's an ideal rose for a small garden. Bred in England by Henry Bennet in 1887, 'Mrs. John Laing' became so sought after that $45,000 was offered for distribution rights in North America, an unheard of sum for a rose in those days. ZONES 5–9

## Paul Ricault
1845, fragrant
Magnificent, rich, rose-pink blooms open flat and often quartered with reflexing center petals. The

Top right: 'Mrs. John Laing'
Right: 'Paul Ricault'

'Reine des Violettes'

'Archduke Joseph'

bush is strong with arching canes. Flowers are usually borne singly on long stems, excellent for picking. ZONES 5–9

### Reine des Violettes

(Queen of the Violets), 1860, fragrant, few thorns
Totally delicious! If you can grow only one Hybrid Perpetual, choose this one. Imagine pink, magenta, lilac and purple pastel crayons all smudged together, then add a pale highlight in the center, and you will have an idea of the color – which is difficult to photograph. Large blooms open flat, quartered and layered with soft petals. The bush is tall, hardy and reasonably disease-resistant, with arching canes and soft gray-green foliage. A relic of the Victorian era of over-stuffed sofas and plum purple velvets. Not recommended for minimalists. ZONES 5–9

## Teas and Early Hybrid Teas

The ancestry of the group christened Tea roses is directly linked to early roses from China, notably 'Hume's Blush' (pale pink) and 'Parks' Yellow' which were themselves the result of much earlier hybridizing by Chinese gardeners or chance crosses between China roses *R. chinensis* and *R. gigantea*.

Other groups of roses became involved but, to put it briefly, Tea roses were bred from pink and yellow Chinese roses and have inherited the long flowering habit, grace and subtle colors of their ancestors. The name Tea was coined because roses were often transported to Europe along with cargoes of tea by the clipper ships of the East India Company. Perhaps the smell of tea clung to the plants when they were unloaded but it is more likely the name referred to their mode of transport. I have never detected a tea fragrance in roses.

In the main, Teas resent hard pruning. It is better to remove dead and spindly wood, prune lightly and deadhead conscientiously. In general, Teas are regarded as tender and not suited to very cold climates.

Early Hybrid Teas evolved primarily from crossing Teas with Hybrid Perpetuals and were the result of hybridizers' attempts to satisfy the public's demand for novelty. "We're tired of fat faces, flat faces and cups. Give us something new and gorgeous that flowers all the time and copes better with cold," they probably said.

The first rose officially recognized as a Hybrid Tea was an elegant silvery pink bred by Jean Baptiste Guillot of Lyon. The winner of a competition at an International Exhibition in 1867, and named 'La France', it showed the high peaked form characteristic of future Hybrid Teas. However, it was difficult to breed from and it wasn't until 1882 when English hybridizer, Henry Bennett, introduced 'Lady

Mary Fitzwilliam', a delightful creamy pink confection, that a fertile parent for future Hybrid Teas was found. Both of these roses are still in the catalogs.

There were no yellow Hybrid Teas until 1900 when another French breeder, Joseph Pernet-Ducher, introduced 'Soleil d'Or' and a little later 'Rayon d'Or' followed by a whole series of variations on yellow.

This was a tremendous achievement somewhat marred by the fact that the roses he used in his breeding program bestowed a susceptibility to black spot on their descendants. Most Teas and Hybrid Teas repeat bloom from spring through to fall.

### Archduke Joseph
1892, Tea
This amazing rose is burnished copper and bronze shot with pink – or orange and russet shot with purple. It's impossible to precisely describe it except to say that instead of looking bizarre, it all works superbly and the big full-petaled blooms are strikingly beautiful. The bush is big, well foliaged and healthy. ZONES 7–9

### Duchesse de Brabant
1857, Tea
One of the most graceful, free-flowering of the Teas. Pearly pink double-cupped blooms cover a tall and vigorous shrubby bush from spring through to winter. Foliage is fresh apple green, healthy and plentiful. ZONES 5–11

### Jean Ducher
1874, Tea, few thorns
Another of my favorite roses. The large flowers are quite distinctive. Layers of peaches-and-cream petals are arranged like layers of loosely folded silk. The bush is tall and shrubby and may need support to carry the weight of its blooms. New shoots and foliage are wine red. In my garden, it is one of the first roses to flower and repeats consistently into winter. One of the hardiest of the Teas, it can stand

Top: 'Jean Ducher'
Above: 'Duchesse de Brabant' in a perennial border.

Top: 'Général Galliéni'
Above: 'Dainty Bess'

more variations in temperature than most and I have seen it still in bud in the snow. Resents hard pruning. ZONES 5–10

### Général Galliéni
1899, Hybrid Tea, few thorns
A remarkable rose of great distinction fittingly named for the French general responsible for the defence of Paris at the beginning of World War I. As the flower opens, it appears that a tight posy of buff yellow rose buds has been crammed into a cup of carmine petals but once the unruly petals unfold, anything can happen. No two roses seem to be the same, and to further complicate things, the big double flowers change colors with the seasons, the situation and the soil. The 'General' blooms from spring to fall when the petals darken to mahogany red. A tall strong branching bush. Plant it and you will never be bored. ZONES 7–9

### Safrano
1839, Tea
One of the early Teas, bred directly from 'Park's Yellow', 'Safrano's' big, informal, semi-double flowers open soft saffron yellow tinged with apricot, fading to buff with age and sun. It was much admired in its day and the lovely buds were considered perfect for buttonholes. A charming custom – bring back the buttonhole! If you like soft pretty roses that fade, it is well worth planting. Wine-tinted young foliage offsets the blooms beautifully and it flowers freely from spring through fall. ZONES 7–9

## Climbing Teas and Hybrid Teas
As with the Teas and Hybrid Teas, most of these climbers bloom right through from spring to fall.

### Dainty Bess
1925, Hybrid Tea, bush and climber
If you think you don't like single roses, 'Dainty Bess' will change your mind. We're looking at the 1920s here with chemise dresses, short skirts and

'Devoniensis'

tea dances. Clusters of long slim buds open to big, dusty-pink, wavy-petaled blooms with golden brown stamens. There is a moderate bush and a climbing form ideal for a pillar or wall.

'Dainty Bess' dies well. The five petals fall and only the lovely stamens remain. ZONES 5–9

### Devoniensis
(Magnolia Rose, Victoria) 1858, Tea, fragrant, few thorns
From pink-tinted buds, big clotted cream blooms open flat and quartered. The velvety texture of the petals and the perfume are reminiscent of *Magnolia grandiflora*. Splendid red-green foliage and new growth highlights the beauty of the blooms.

There are bush and climbing forms but I recommend the climber. Repeats well. ZONES 6–11

### Gloire de Dijon
1853, Tea, fragrant
Big full flowers of this much-loved rose open flat with silky crumpled and quartered petals. Color can vary from copper, through pale yellow, peachy pink and buff. Author H.E. Bates compares them to "a creamy elegant bosom, slightly flushed" but you can't depend on it. It's a wonderful rose – breathtakingly beautiful on an old brick or mellow stone wall

Right: 'Gloire de Dijon'

for instance – and surprisingly cold hardy – but in my experience it needs extra care to ward off diseases. ZONES 5–9

### Lady Hillingdon
1917, Tea, few thorns
Yes, I know she's inclined to hang her head but that can be a virtue in a climber.

Long, elegant, pointed apricot buds open to nodding, buff-apricot, semi-double flowers beautifully displayed on bronze stems among plum-colored foliage. Flowers early and repeats through fall in a warm spot. The plant is often slow to grow initially but be patient – it's worth it. ZONES 5–10

### Mme. Caroline Testout
(City of Portland) 1901, Hybrid Tea, fragrant
Big satiny pink blooms on strong stems are goblet-shaped with rolled edges to the petals. A bush form of the rose was bred in 1890 by French hybridizer Joseph Pernet-Ducher who was not impressed with it as a seedling but along came Mme. Caroline Testout, a dressmaker with an eye for an advertising gimmick. She bought it, named it after herself and launched it at her showrooms in the spring of 1890. The rose became popular and her salons prospered,

Above: 'Souvenir de Mme. Léonie Viennot'
Left: 'Sombreuil'

always decorated lavishly with her own rose. A vigorous climbing sport was introduced in 1901. It's a reliable, profuse and recurrent bloomer with good foliage. ZONES 5–11

### Sombreuil
(Mlle de Sombreuil, Colonial White), Tea, fragrant
The flowers are exquisite – they are the color of

old ivory – crammed with petals, often quilled and quartered, opening flat to show a button eye. Although the stems are thorny, it's a manageable climber on a wall – or over a pergola for maximum effect. Dark green foliage offsets the blooms beautifully. Repeats well. Mlle de Sombreuil was a heroine of the French Revolution who saved her father from the guillotine. ZONES 7–9

### Souvenir de Mme. Léonie Viennot
1898, Tea
It doesn't have much of a perfume and the flowers aren't really pickable but in the garden this is one of the most gorgeous climbers you could imagine – a luscious, big, sprawling climber for a warm spot. Loose informal blooms are sun-kissed apricot and coppery pink. Long pointed leaves, an inheritance from *R. gigantea*, make it easily recognizable.

It blooms better if left largely unpruned except for the removal of dead wood. I grow it on a fence along the sunny bank of a stream where it looks after itself. Perfect for a wall or up a tree. ZONES 7–9

## Hybrid Musks
Roses and the country clergy seem to have an affinity for each other. Perhaps these rural reverend gentlemen, having dealt with the Sunday sermon, had time for the purest of pleasures. An English country clergyman, the Reverend Joseph Pemberton, is credited with the introduction of a group of hardy, disease-resistant, long-flowering roses which became known as Hybrid Musks, although their connection with the Musk Rose (*R. moschata*) is marginal. When Pemberton died in 1925, his sister Florence carried on hybridizing for a short time and then the entire collection of roses was handed over to the Pembertons' gardeners, Anne and John Bentall, who introduced more Hybrid Musks.

As these roses were largely released in the 1920s and 30s, they are not quite "old" roses but because

of their form, fragrance and bushy, spreading habit of growth, they are usually included in "old rose" literature – and in the gardens of old rose enthusiasts.

Hybrid Musks are most likely to be tall strong shrubs, uniformly beautiful, robust and not given to displays of temperament. You really can't go wrong with them. Most Hybrid Musks flower from spring through to fall.

The great German nursery of the Kordes family has added many excellent varieties.

### Ballerina
1937, shrub-climber
Ann Bentall discovered this rose as a chance seedling. Although her husband never thought much of it, Ann persisted and the well-named 'Ballerina' was introduced to become an immediate success. In late spring, 'Ballerina' bursts into blossoms that last until late fall. Individual flowers are small and dainty singles, carmine pink at the edge of the petals

Right: 'Ballerina'

Above: 'Cornelia'
Left: 'Buff Beauty'

shading to white in the center. They are borne in enormous sprays.

Grown as a shrub, 'Ballerina' forms a spreading mound with branches arching to the ground. It makes a very pretty climber trained around a window and an excellent bridge between other roses in a border. Use it as a hedging rose or grow it in informal mounds near water. ZONES 4–9

## Buff Beauty
1939, shrub-climber
You have to love this rose. Deep apricot buds open to full-petaled, frilly, pale apricot blooms that fade to buff. In a dry fall, blooms may a have a pink tinge.

The bush is well foliaged and tall, better with support – or you can grow it as a climber.

It's a rose that appreciates being looked up to because its blooms are inclined to hang down with the weight of the petals. ZONES 4–9

## Cornelia
1925, fragrant, shrub-climber, few thorns
Arching branches are covered with big luscious sprays of small flowers with layers of coral pink petals and golden stamens. Its Musk rose fragrance has been described as a mixture of heliotrope and narcissus. Grow it as a big shrub or train it over an arch, an arbor or a wall. It flowers consistently and will delight you however you use it. ZONES 4–9

## Moonlight
1913
One of Pemberton's early roses, and one of the best. Clusters of small, semi-double blooms are ivory tinged with lemon and have prominent yellow stamens. Glossy, dark green foliage makes an excellent frame for the pale flowers which begin in spring and continue through fall. Hardy, reliable and disease-resistant, 'Moonlight' is a pleasant change from busty beauties and the longer you grow it, the more it appeals. Makes the perfect hedge. Try it against red bricks. ZONES 4–11

## Penelope
1924, shrub-climber
Sheer delight. The spreading shrub covered with

Above left: 'Penelope'
Above: 'Ghislaine de Féligonde'
Left: 'Moonlight' (left) and Noisette rose 'Lamarque' (right).

are not exceptional, but the graceful airy habit of growth of the bush, with its vibrant flowers on long stems, makes sure it is noticed. Long flowering and hardy, it's a good plant for the back of a border as a contrast to paler pinks. ZONES 4–9

## Shrubs, shrub-climbers and ramblers

There are a number of roses, large and small, that are difficult to categorize adequately in a small book but much too good to leave out.

### Ghislaine de Féligonde
1916, shrub-rambler
('Helenn' is an approximate pronunciation)
A terrific rose that can be grown as a big arching shrub or a moderate rambler, and will cope with poor soil, sun or shade. Clusters of deep orange buds open to smallish double flowers that can be apricots and cream or pinkish terracotta with a flick of yellow. Expect big flushes of blooms in spring and again in fall. Foliage is glossy, tough, pest-free and disease-resistant. This rose is named for a Flemish heroine of World War I who rescued her wounded husband, Comte de Féligonde, from the battlefield. ZONES 6–9

clusters of big, wide-open, semi-double flowers of mother-of-pearl and shell pink with wavy-edged petals is instantly recognizable in the garden. Habit of growth is graceful and new foliage and stems are plum red. Don't deadhead for too long and you will get handsome hips in late fall. A substantial hedge rose or a specimen shrub. Cold hardy and disease-resistant. ZONES 4–11

### Vanity
1920, fragrant, shrub-climber
A tall open bush or small climber with masses of rich, cerise, semi-single flowers which themselves

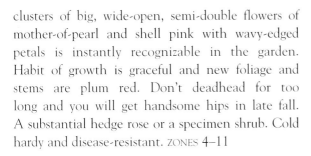

Above left: 'Gruss an Aachen'
Above right: 'May Queen'
Left: 'Stanwell Perpetual'

## Gruss an Aachen

(Salut d'Aix la Chapelle), 1909

Indispensable for a small garden – or any garden – this amiable and romantic peaches-and-cream rose blooms from spring to winter on a compact, floribunda-type bush. Big flowers are luscious doubles packed with petals, opening flat. Disease-resistant. ZONES 4–9

## May Queen

1898, shrub-rambler

This underrated rose should be grown more. Medium-sized double flowers packed with prettily crumpled petals are deep pink at the center, paling on the outer edges. Healthy glossy leaves will stay on through mild winters. It will form a large sprawling mound to cover banks or will climb if encouraged. My own 'May Queen' falls in flowery loops from the top of a tree. Train it over a fence to make a dense shiny hedge. This rose has a big spring/summer flowering and later intermittent blooms. ZONES 4–9

## Mermaid

1918

Grow it if you have the space – and the constitution. 'Mermaid' is gorgeous but about as far from voluptuous over-stuffed Victoriana as you could get. If you are still reading, flowers are huge, single and palest yellow with amber stamens, lovely even when the petals fall. There's a coppery glint to the young, almost evergreen leaves. Everything about 'Mermaid' seems to glisten like the sun on water. But it is horrendously, wickedly thorny and in a warm climate its rampant canes can gobble up houses, given a chance. Grow it where it will never – well, hardly ever – need to be pruned. It gives you a continuous flowering through the summer. ZONES 7–11

## New Dawn

(Ever-blooming Dr. Van Fleet), 1930

Introduced by a Connecticut nursery, it became one

of the world's most popular roses. Loosely double flowers are soft creamy pink, foliage is glossy and disease-resistant, growth is vigorous and canes are very thorny. It flowers profusely in early summer and is capable of flowering continuously – but don't expect that first, fine, careless rapture.

It has made an excellent parent and features in the breeding of many good roses. 'Awakening', an excellent sport, has the color and constitution of 'New Dawn' but flowers have many more petals and a sumptuous double and quartered old-fashioned form. ZONES 4–10

## Paul Transon
### 1900, shrub-rambler
A rose with style, and instantly recognizable by its form and color. Flowers are large for a rambler with concentric rows of pointed petals, shorter in the center, a bit like a disheveled dahlia. From coppery buds, flowers open washed terra-cotta pink, sometimes dark, sometimes pale. Shiny healthy foliage. A big spring/early summer display, a few repeats, then fall flowers in a good year. Can be grown as a big sprawling shrub or climber. ZONES 4–9

## Phyllis Bide
### 1923, shrub-climber
Semi-double flowers – tinted peaches-and-cream, pink and primrose, but not entirely any of those colors – it seems to have been delicately painted with a fine brush. Foliage is small but plentiful and growth is airy and easily trained. With 'Perle d'Or' and 'Gloire de Dijon' as parents, you would expect a superb rose. If you want a big bush or a mannerly climber with non-stop flowers that don't overwhelm, you couldn't do better. Lovely trained up pillars, along a fence or veranda rail – or grown as a weeping standard. It flowers from spring to fall. ZONES 4–9

## Stanwell Perpetual
### 1838
Big, flesh-pink, fully double flowers open flat, quilled and folded to show golden stamens and seem much too delicately pretty for the rugged bush. A natural hybrid of a 'Pimpinellifolia' ('Scots') rose and 'The Fall Damask', this is a prickly shrub but that's forgivable in a bush that produces such beautiful flowers continuously from spring to fall. Foliage is ferny and flowers are borne all along arching canes. Several bushes planted together will eventually form a huge flowery mound – or make an excellent hardy hedge. ZONES 4–9

## Rugosas
Rugosa roses are ferociously prickly but that doesn't matter because you will prune them only when they grow too big for their situation. I mention the prickles first because every other attribute is in their favor. This remarkable group with wrinkled (rugose) leaves, quite unlike conventional rose foliage, are natives of Northern China and Japan. They were introduced into Europe in 1784 by Swedish botanist,

'Agnes'

Carl Thunberg, but because they did not resemble the accepted idea of roses and the blooms would win no prizes at shows, they were largely ignored for a hundred years.

From the late 19th century their popularity has increased and today they are recognized as hardy and rewarding shrubs with the most beautiful and aristocratic of flowers.

Rugosas will thrive where other roses would die. They cope with poor soil, hot summers, bitter winters and strong winds. These are the roses that color the sandy shore of the northeast coast of America and perfume the air for miles around until a gale blows in from the sea and strips their petals in a day. In Europe they soften the edges of busy highways and fill guardrails where they thrive on pollution.

Dark green, deeply veined leaves can turn butter yellow and russet in fall – don't think your plant is dying! And no aphid in its right mind would touch them. Except for a few over-gently bred modern hybrids, they are disease-free.

Now we come to the best part – the flowers, fragrance and hips the size of crabapples! Big, airy, single, semi-double, double, ruffled and sumptuous flowers full of perfume will delight you from spring through to fall, and the pleasure continues with huge and brilliant fall hips from single varieties.

## Agnes
1922, fragrant
A fully double and fragrant pale amber rose with soft frilly petals and a deceptively delicate air, 'Agnes' was bred in Canada and can cope with extremes of weather.

The bush grows quickly to 6 to 10 ft. (2 to 3 m). A profuse flowering in spring/summer and repeat blooms in a warm fall. ZONES 3–9

## *R. rugosa alba*
1870
Long, pointed, blush-tinted buds open to big, hibiscus-like, single flowers, immaculately white with a bright coronet of golden stamens – one of the most beautiful of all single roses. Flowers continue through summer and fall when foliage turns butter-yellow. At this point, if you haven't deadheaded (I never deadhead rugosas) you get bunches of big tomato-red hips, a lovely contrast to continuing

*R. rugosa alba*

'Blanc Double de Coubert'

flowers. You can depend upon a robust spreading shrub to about 6½ ft. (2 m) given time – excellent as a specimen or a hedge. ZONES 3–10

## Belle Poitevine
1894
Big, semi-double, rose-pink flowers tinted mauve open from characteristic long buds. Foliage is dark green and the bush is upright and tall. As a bonus, the bush occasionally sets big wine-colored hips, unusual in a double variety. ZONES 4–9

## Blanc Double de Coubert
1892, very fragrant
An exceptionally beautiful double white rose, sometimes called the 'Muslin Rose' because of the airy transparency of its petals. It grows to a big shrub, occasionally sets hips and makes a tough and wonderfully fragrant hedge. The petals are so fine, they flop in persistent rain, but the blooms are so lovely who cares? ZONES 4–9

## Frau Dagmar Hastrup
1914
Huge single flowers are clear pink with delicate but

noticeable veining and amber stamens. Inclined to be low-growing and spreading, it continues to flower while it sets enormous tomato-shaped hips that turn a glossy mulberry in the fall. Sometimes slow to grow initially but be patient. It's worth it. ZONES 4–9

## Hansa
1905, very fragrant
Big loosely double blooms are a vivid magenta-pink, tinted with violet and heavily fragrant. My bushes grow in stony soil to perfume the air and lift the spirits along a driveway. Many roses are fragrant if you bury your nose in the petals but cannot waft their fragrance over a distance. ZONES 4–9

'Frau Dagmar Hastrup'

'Roseraie de l'Hay'

### Roseraie de l'Hay
1901, very fragrant

Named for the famous French rose garden, this is a glorious Rugosa. Big peony-like blooms are iridescent, velvety crimson-purple – a bit like an improved version of 'Hansa', I suppose. The spicy perfume has been compared to sugared almonds but to me it's more like clove-scented dianthus. Whatever the description, it's delicious. ZONES 4–9

### Souvenir de Philemon Cochet
1899, very fragrant

Like a double white hollyhock, this sport of 'Blanc Double de Coubert' opens flat and frilly with a ruffle of petaloids in the center. It does not flower as generously as its parent, but it's an exquisite rose. Grow them together in a hedge. ZONES 4–10

'Souvenir de Philemon Cochet'

# CHAPTER 4

# *David Austin Roses*

Until the advent of David Austin's English roses, modern rose growing had made slow progress along stereotyped lines with the emphasis firmly on Hybrid Teas. A change in direction was long overdue. David Austin achieved that change with the biggest advance in rose hybridization in a hundred years.

For thousands of years, rose species and the resulting hybrids interbred in the wild. Humans had nothing to do with it. There they were, untouched by human hand and perhaps that's part of the charm of the species and their near hybrids we still grow today. When we perfected the techniques of hand pollination, the way was open for new specific groups of roses and the cat was well and truly out of the bag.

Let's fast-forward to comparatively recent rose history. The momentous discovery of the repeat-flowering China rose in the 18th century enabled hybridizers to introduce new classes of repeat-flowering roses so that by the beginning of the 19th century there had been a shift in popularity from the old, once-flowering European roses to the repeat-flowering Bourbons, Noisettes, Hybrid Perpetuals and Teas.

However, when Hybrid Teas were introduced later that century, their success dominated the rose world and stopped any further development of the old European lines for more than a hundred years.

In the late 20th century, David Austin turned the rose world upside down. Put briefly, his method was to go back to 1800 and invest the old European rose with the desirable attributes of recurrent

'Grace'

flowering and the yellow tones found in Noisettes without losing any of the old-fashioned virtues of flower form, fragrance and graceful habit of growth.

Unlike many illustrious hybridizers of the past, he does not belong to a rose-breeding dynasty but comes from an old, established farming family in Shropshire, England. It was an historical tragedy that turned what might have been a hobby into a career.

During World War II, most of the land on his father's farm was requisitioned to be used as an air base. When the war ended there was not enough workable land left to make an economic farming unit and the young David's thoughts turned to horticulture, which had always been an interest, and to roses in particular. To this end, he worked

'William Morris'

for a time at Sunningdale Nursery and it was here that he met England's famous rosarian and author, Graham Stuart Thomas, who became a lifelong friend. Although he returned to farming, the breeding of new roses became a consuming interest. He had a great affection for the old, once-flowering shrub roses and dreamed of creating a new race of perpetual flowering shrub roses by crossing these old roses with modern Hybrid Teas and Floribundas.

Throughout the 1950s he made many crosses but his first success came in 1961 with 'Constance Spry', the lusty and sumptuous rose pink offspring of 'Dainty Maid', a modern Floribunda (1940) and the old Gallica rose 'Belle Isis' (1845). It scored highly in color, flower, perfume and vigor but it was a sprawling shrub-climber that flowered only once in spring. More hybridization was needed to get the rose David Austin wanted.

'Constance Spry' was crossed with other pink, repeat-flowering roses – the Floribunda 'Ma Perkins' with cupped flowers of salmon, shell pink and cream; the Hybrid Tea 'Monique' for its exquisite mix of pinks; the robust old Hybrid Tea 'Mme. Caroline Testout' with full cupped blooms of an even silvery pink. In this way, the pink coloring was established.

A few years later in 1967, a cross between the Floribunda 'Dusky Maiden' and the old deep crimson Gallica 'Tuscany' resulted in the wine red 'Chianti'. To establish the red color in English roses, further crosses were made which included the parent of unfading red roses, 'Chateau de Clos Vougeot', a superbly scented early Hybrid Tea.

Although both are once-flowering, 'Contance Spry' and 'Chianti' represented the beginning of English roses. The stage was set for David Austin to cross and recross their progeny, introducing other roses to secure shrubby growth, a variety of flower forms and colors and a reliable, repeat-flowering habit. Roses used in the breeding included the climbers 'Aloha' and 'Parade' to increase vigor and a free-flowering habit, the Floribunda 'Chinatown' and the big tough butterfly single 'Golden Wings' to bring in shades of yellow. To provide almost every virtue known to nurserymen, he used the universally popular 'Iceberg'.

There were old roses of course, among them 'Comte de Chambord', 'Duchesse de Montebello', 'Louise Odier', 'Alister Stella Gray', 'Mme. Legras de St. Germain', as well as 'Conrad Ferdinand Meyer' – a tough thorny Rugosa hybrid with the glorious roses 'Gloire de Dijon' and 'Souvenir de la Malmaison' in its ancestry.

David Austin makes it clear he did not set out to produce reproduction old roses but rather a group he describes as "broadly in the mood of old roses." These objectives were to achieve:

- The many flower formations of old roses as opposed to the simple bud formation of the Hybrid Tea.
- A discernable and pleasing fragrance.
- A shrubby plant with good foliage.
- A repeat-flowering habit.
- Strength and disease-resistance.

Since the 1970s when the first roses created a sensation, hundreds of English roses have been introduced

Above: 'Constance Spry'
Right: 'William Shakespeare 2000'

and new ones appear each year. Although only a minuscule percentage of the many thousands of seedlings grown each year is developed commercially, it follows that not all of the roses introduced will have all of the prescribed virtues. There would not be many of us around if each of us were expected to be perfect in every way. Fortunately, we are not cut down and culled as ruthlessly as David Austin's roses. He is quick to eliminate roses from his catalog if he feels they have been superseded by better ones. I suppose that is inevitable if you are producing hundreds of roses over 40 years, but admitting it shows honesty and dedication to task on the part of the breeder. (Many of the roses no longer on his list are well worth growing and still available in nurseries.) David Austin's aim is always to produce better roses in every way but more particularly with resistance to disease.

English roses as a group are considered to be shrub roses, but habit of growth varies and among them you will find roses that are small and compact, tall and upright, wide and arching, low and ground covering, shrub-climbers and climbers. Habit of growth can vary according to climate. Some roses that sit primly in a border and grow to only 3 ft. (1 m) in cold climates can throw off their inhibitions and throw out long canes, heavy with flowers, to

'Brother Cadfael'

reach 6 to 9 ft. (2–3 m) in warm climates. Where this is likely, it will be mentioned in the text.

Fragrance is an important and interesting attribute in English roses. I find they have four main fragrances: traditional heavy old rose, lighter scent of Tea rose, fresh citrus and the unmistakable scent of honey mixed with incense that their breeder calls "myrrh." The dictionary defines myrrh as "an aromatic resin from trees grown in Arabia and Abyssinia, used in the manufacture of perfumes and incense." And if that doesn't make you think of an exotic, incense-laden perfume on a warm wind, you have no romance in your soul.

The colors of English roses can be rich and dark, pale and delicate and everything in between. Roses

with apricot and pink in their petals, a mix which David Austin does so well, often have a lovely luminous quality as if the flowers were lit from within. He writes, "Mere multiplication of colors is not necessarily desirable in itself; the important thing is that the colors should be good colors, and colors suitable to roses. In the modern rose, colors have too frequently tended to be harsh and metallic in appearance. With the English roses, we have returned to softer and sometimes richer shades, which seem to us to be more in keeping with the spirit of the rose."

In the main, English roses are romantic roses – fragrant, sumptuous, silky petaled and exquisitely colored – but they are modern roses and should be given the same care we would give to Floribundas and Hybrid Teas. This means they should be planted in good soil in a sunny place, watered, fed, pruned and sprayed if necessary. It isn't much to ask for the rewards we get.

A few of the hundreds available are listed below. Roses that can be grown as moderate climbers ideal for walls, arches, pillars, etc., will be referred to as shrub-climbers in the text. To keep them flowering from top to base, David Austin recommends either fanning the stems out (for a wall) or pruning one or two of the main stems lower than others (for arches and pillars). Unless mentioned otherwise in the list below, David Austin roses flower from spring through to fall.

### Abraham Darby

(Abraham, Country Darby), fragrant

What do you get when you cross a yellow rose ('Chinatown') and a deep pink rose ('Aloha')? In this case you get creamy pink petals surrounding a mass of petals, peachy pink on the inside, glistening pale yellow on the reverse. It may sound like a fruit salad but, as in many English roses, the combination of colors in the fluted petals produces a luminous quality that is strikingly beautiful: a rose in the soft glow of lamplight in an old painting perhaps.

The rose is very large and deeply cupped, with heavy petals, but in no way clumsy and is complemented by shiny, substantial, healthy foliage. Large blooms suit the vigorous bush which can be grown as a big spreading shrub – or a moderate climber in warm climates. ZONES 4–9

## Ambridge Rose

Cupped, double flowers opening to rosette form are deep apricot in the center, paling to apricots and cream around the edges. Moderate upright growth and a tough healthy shrub. ZONES 4–9

## A Shropshire Lad

fruity fragrance

Flowers are particularly beautiful with soft, peach pink petals in a rosette form within a shallow cup. A robust, tall and reliable shrub related to 'Leander' from which it inherits its vigor and health, it can also be grown as a shrub-climber. ZONES 4–10

## Belle Story

One of David Austin's early roses and in my opinion one of the best. It is an ongoing delight to watch the elegant way this rose opens and I love its semi-double peony form. Big flowers in clusters open wide to a perfectly symmetrical shallow cup. The opening rose is a luminous peach with a big boss of long golden stamens, but as the flower ages, the petals relax and fade to a soft pink and the stamens turn to amber tipped with brown. The bush is tall, vigorous and healthy but with an awkward habit of growth. David Austin suggests growing three plants in a triangle for maximum effect. ZONES 4–9

## Blythe Spirit

This rose is very well named. The big informal sprays of soft yellow, frilly flowers cover the bush

Top right: 'Ambridge Rose'
Center right: 'A Shropshire Lad'
Bottom right: 'Belle Story'

'Blythe Spirit'

'Crown Princess Margareta'

from spring right through to the fall. It is the sort of rose that would settle in anywhere. Clever gardeners should go out and buy it immediately because it is claimed to be completely disease-resistant. ZONES 4–9

### Brother Cadfael
fragrant
This is a rose you cannot overlook. Huge, clear pink, double flowers like peonies, deeply cupped and full of petals but never clumsy, are held on a substantial shrub with good foliage so that everything is in proportion. It's a breathtaking rose with a rich, old rose fragrance. ZONES 4–9

### Charlotte
fragrant
Layers of soft, true yellow petals curve inwards to form a cup framed by paler outer petals. One of the prettiest and hardiest of yellow roses, a descendant of the great 'Graham Thomas'. Growth is upright and compact. ZONES 4–9

### Chianti
fragrant
This is one of the original Austin roses and flowers only once in spring but it is still widely grown because it flowers prolifically and a big bush in bloom is a sight to remember. Blooms are large, fully double and the deepest, darkest, wine red with hints of purple as the flower ages. The bush is robust and shrubby and will grow to more than 6½ ft. (2 m). ZONES 4–9

### Comte de Champagne
myrrh fragrance
Semi-double, cupped blooms open rich yellow and gradually fade to champagne as they reveal prominent amber stamens. Flowers are borne on slender arching stems on a wide bushy shrub.

Named after Thibaut IV, the Count of Champagne and Brie who was an ancestor of the President of Taittinger, the makers of the finest champagne – and who introduced *R. gallica officinalis* from Damascus on his return from the seventh Crusade in 1250. ZONES 4–9

## Constance Spry

very fragrant

This important rose that represents the beginning of English roses is big, beautiful and beguiling. Soft, rose pink petals with a luminous quality curl into sumptuous double blooms, perfect for a garden party hat. There is only one summer flowering but it is generous, lasts a long time and you would not easily miss it. Constance flings her prickly canes over everything in sight. Can be grown as a large rampageous bush or a climber but give her plenty of space. ZONES 4–9

## Cottage Rose

David Austin writes, "If you are looking for a good garden rose of truly Old Rose character, that will flower continually throughout the summer, this rose would be hard to better." Medium-sized blooms full of ruffled petals in a shallow cup are warm pink and growth habit is moderate and bushy. A reliable, charming rose suitable for a small garden. ZONES 4–9

## Crown Princess Margareta

fruity fragrance

Big full-petaled rosettes within shallow cups are typical of the form of many English roses, but this one demands attention for its color – a brilliant apricot orange. It is a tall, strong shrub that will climb with encouragement. This rose is named for Crown Princess Margareta of Sweden, a granddaughter of Queen Victoria. She was an accomplished landscape gardener and created the famous Swedish Summer Palace of Sofiero in Helsinborg. ZONES 4–9

## Dapple Dawn

Huge, airy, single flowers are gossamer pink veined with strawberry and paling in the centers to highlight golden stamens. The big tough and healthy sprawling shrub flowers abundantly. Plant as a group for maximum effect or use as a moderate climber.

'Dapple Dawn' is a sport of 'Red Coat', described later in the text, and surprisingly the two roses look fabulous planted together. Grow them with *Verbena bonariensis*. ZONES 4–9

## Eglantyne

(Eglantyne Jebb)

Saucers of pale pink flowers filled with slightly fluted petals, paling to almost white around the edges, make this an exceptionally pretty rose. The plant is

'Charlotte'

'Eglantyne'

well foliaged, twiggy and bushy, disease-resistant and of moderate size. ZONES 4–9

### Evelyn
**very fragrant**
Magnificent cups of silky apricot and pink petals lit with soft yellow in a quartered, old-fashioned form. A strong, upright, bushy shrub named for the perfumers Crabtree & Evelyn. ZONES 4–9

### Fair Bianca
**myrrh fragrance**
The first of David Austin's white roses and still the prettiest in my opinion. Pink buds open to full, flat and quartered blooms in the old-fashioned style, sometimes showing a green eye like the delicious old Damask, 'Mme. Hardy', which it resembles.

Blooms can be tinged with buff in the center in fall but that's an appropriate color for the season. Given good conditions in a warm climate, the bush will grow tall and throw out long canes – all covered with flowers. ZONES 4–9

### Falstaff
**very fragrant**
Big, cupped, full-petaled blooms of darkest crimson tinged with purple and a strong old rose fragrance make this a sumptuous rose. A tall bushy plant that makes a superb shrub-climber. ZONES 4–9

### Gertrude Jekyll
**very fragrant**
Little scrolled buds open to big, fat, warm pink roses that smell divine and are substantial enough to hold their form whatever the weather. Bred from the old Portland rose, 'Comte de Chambord', and named for the great English garden writer, this rose is a delight to have in the garden. The flowers are so fragrant

Top left: 'Evelyn'
Center left: 'Falstaff'
Bottom left: 'Golden Celebration'

they were used for the first rose essence produced in England for 250 years. What's more, the bush is tall, strong, well foliaged, healthy and can be grown as a shrub-climber. ZONES 4–9

### Glamis Castle

Not lush and heavy, but beautifully formed and elegant, pure white blooms open wide to shallow cups of about 40 petals. A manageable, twiggy habit of growth and long and prolific flowering add to its virtues. Considered by many to be the best white English rose. ZONES 4–9

### Golden Celebration

fragrant

The huge, cupped, many-petaled deep golden yellow blooms are said to smell of sauterne wine and strawberries. How's that for a bit of decadence in the garden? Its habit of growth is slightly arching to form a rounded shrub. Glowing flowers are well displayed against ample dark green foliage. ZONES 4–9

### Grace

fragrant

A mass of pure apricot petals, dark in the middle but pale around the outside, in a shallow cup opening to a big rosette, make a beautiful rose. A healthy shrub of moderate size that repeats well. One of David Austin's recent introductions, which he describes as "an excellent garden plant." ZONES 4–9

### Graham Thomas

High, wide and handsome describes 'Graham Thomas'. Clear sunshine yellow blooms are loosely cupped doubles and you can expect a lot of them. Borne on long stems, they are excellent for picking and last well in the bud. In warm areas, 'Graham Thomas' has been known to bloom all through a mild winter. It also far exceeds the height initially given by its breeder which was a moderate 3¾ ft. (1.2 m). In a temperate climate, you can expect a big shrub-climber capable of growing to 10 ft. (3 m)

'Graham Thomas'

or more. If you have space for a robust and reliable yellow shrub rose that will light up your garden, this is it.

Try underplanting it with electric blue delphiniums or larkspurs and cranesbill *Geranium* 'Johnson's Blue'. The rose is named for the famous English rosarian and author. ZONES 4–9

### Happy Child

Big cups of deepest yellow are beautifully offset by big polished camellia-like leaves. Moderate arching growth on an attractive all-rounder. ZONES 4–9

### Heritage

fragrant

Ten years ago I wrote, "In elegance, color and delicacy of form, this rose is beyond compare." I wouldn't go quite so far over the top today, but it is still one of my favorite English roses. Big flowers are porcelain pink with a mother-of-pearl sheen on petals precisely curved within a cup and borne on long-stemmed sprays. They remind me of the exquisite blooms of an early 19th-century Gallica rose, 'Duchesse de Montebello', which is used in the breeding.

The continuity of flowering from spring through to fall is excellent and the bush is moderate to tall with good foliage and a reasonably compact habit of growth. ZONES 4–9

'Kathryn Morley'

'John Clare'

### Jacquenetta

If you like single roses, you will love this one. Large, semi-single, wavy-petaled blooms are a beautiful blending of apricot and pink, sometimes borne in clusters, sometimes singly. The moderate bush is healthy and long flowering. Appropriately named for a simple country wench in Shakespeare's *Love's Labour's Lost*. ZONES 4–9

### John Clare

The breeder claims this is one of the most prolific of English roses, bearing its medium-sized, cupped, pink flowers with remarkable continuity throughout summer and putting on a spectacular show in fall. Growth is moderate. ZONES 4–9

### Kathryn Morley

fragrant

The petal form of this rose is enchanting. Pale pink, inner petals intertwine and outer petals reflex to frame them. The bush, though robust, is awkward with a mix of long and short canes but the beauty of the flowers compensates. ZONES 4–9

### L.D. Braithwaite

fragrant when it ages

Its breeder says it has the brightest crimson coloring

'L.D. Braithwaite'

'Leander'

of all English roses. I've heard it described as his best red rose, although not the most luscious. It has very desirable virtues though. Big, double, sometimes quartered blooms hold their rich coloring and do not fade or burn in the sun as some red roses do. They also stand up well in wet weather. Continuity of flowering is excellent and growth is moderate and healthy. A good rose for mass planting. ZONES 4–9

## Leander
myrrh fragrance
Throughout spring and summer, 'Leander' is a terrific rose and if you remember to cut it back and feed it after its first big flush in summer you will probably – but not certainly – get fall blooms as well. Picture a big, strong shrub well clothed with dark green leaves and with all its sturdy branches laden with sprays of perfect roses. Tight, bright apricot buds open wide and almost flat to a symmetrical old rose form, quartered in the center, with each petal precisely in place. A little too perfect perhaps?

The color? Well, it's apricot mousse, apricots with whipped cream, and finally powder puff pink as the flower ages. 'Leander' is the 'Buff Beauty' of English roses and can produce apricot, buff and pale pink blooms at the same time, particularly in fall.

Who could refuse a handsome, disease-resistant

shrub-climber with very few thorns and flowers that smell of honey and warm incense-laden winds – particularly when it's named for the mythological youth who nightly swam the Hellespont to visit Hero, a priestess of Venus? ZONES 4–9

## Lucetta
Peaches-and-cream flowers with a velvety quality are large, loosely double with prominent gold/amber stamens and held prettily in clusters. The bush is tough, tall and spreading with long arching branches. Grown against a trellis, arch or pillar, it can be treated as a climber and will tolerate a reasonable amount of shade. ZONES 4–10

## Mary Rose
An early English rose that has remained universally popular. Fully double blooms, borne in abundance, are clear rose pink, not heart-stoppingly beautiful but always reliably there. The well-foliaged bush is moderate in size, nicely shrubby, tough, twiggy and easy to control. The breeder describes it as "in every way a good garden plant." ZONES 4–9

## Miss Alice
fragrant
A totally enchanting rose. Soft pink, incurving

petals in the center, sometimes quartered, are framed by paler petals around the outside. They are not huge but substantial – about 3½–4 in. (9–10 cm) across – and in good proportion to the short but bushy plant, perfect for the front of a border or in a bed. Named for Miss Alice de Rothschild who created the rose garden at Waddesdon Manor in England. ZONES 4–9

### Molyneux
fragrant
Double rosettes of flowers the color of farm-fresh egg yolks cover a moderately low-growing, disease-resistant, shrubby bush. This multiple award winner is an excellent rose for growing in beds and the front of borders. ZONES 4–9

### Morning Mist
Grow this rose if you have the space to let it fling out its thorny canes and form a big shrub. Carried in

Top: 'Morning Mist'
Above: 'Molyneux'

substantial clusters on tall stems, the single flowers are magnificent. From pointed, orange flame buds, big five-petaled flowers open washed terra-cotta pink, shaded gold in the center where they meet a curly mop of gold and deep terra-cotta stamens. The bush is vigorous and healthy. Fall repeats are particularly good. ZONES 4–9

## Pat Austin

fragrant

A vibrant rose named after David Austin's wife and a new color for English roses – bright copper on the inside of the petals, pale coppery yellow on the outside.

Flowers are fully double and deeply cupped so that dark and pale shades are visible at the same time as the flower opens. Foliage is plentiful and habit of growth is strong and shrubby, similar to 'Abraham Darby'. An eye-catcher in a border. ZONES 4–9

## Pretty Jessica

very fragrant

Sumptuous, warm pink, goblet-shaped blooms, heavy with petals, open to big, shallow cups. In form and color 'Pretty Jessica' is reminiscent of Centifolias, the old cabbage roses often featured in paintings. Blooming is continuous from spring to fall although fat buds are inclined to ball in wet weather. The bush is upright, pleasantly bushy and moderate enough in height to suit a small garden. Watch out for black spot but don't let it deter you from growing this charmer. ZONES 4–9

## Red Coat

A cheerful, uncomplicated, single, fire-engine red rose that flowers forever. Well, almost. 'Redcoat' will flower through four seasons in warm areas. Masses of very large flowers like fluttering butterflies open wide to display prominent yellow stamens. This is a marvelous rose to use as a hedge or plant *en masse*. The bush is tall, tough, vigorous and disease-resistant. ZONES 4–9

## Sharifa Asma

This rose has been around since 1989 and its breeder, who is quick to cull those he considers not up to standard, still considers it one of his best. Flowers are breathtakingly beautiful in that big, full-petaled, shallow-cup-reflexing-to-a-rosette form that David Austin does so well. Coloring could not

Top: 'Pretty Jessica'
Above: 'Red Coat'

be more delicate – rose pink in the center paling to blush around the outside or entirely creamy blush. It is said to smell of white grapes and mulberry. Nearly 10 years ago I wrote, "Something is lacking. They seem out of proportion to the comparatively small bush. They seem lovely, but a novelty. Time will tell." It has – and I was wrong. ZONES 4–10

## Shropshire Lass

Introduced in 1968 and one of its breeder's first successes, this rose is still in his catalogs because it has so many virtues. What do you get when you cross the Hybrid Tea 'Madame Butterfly' with the glorious old Alba 'Mme. Legras de St. Germain'? If you're David Austin, you get the exquisite 'Shropshire Lass' which sounds like a draught horse but looks like fine porcelain. From pointed, pale pink buds, the flowers open a milky blush, very large and a little more than single with a mass of golden stamens and a gauzy, translucent quality. Who cares if it flowers only in summer? Among a border of buxom beauties, it will be the one your friends notice and drool over. Did I mention it is hardy, shade tolerant, disease-resistant and happy to form a big but compact shrub or climb if encouraged? ZONES 4–10

### Sweet Juliet

Apricot and gold buds open to layered rosettes, deep apricot in the center with a button eye, petals paling to cream and a tracery of apricot veining. Beautiful flowers on a strong-growing, reliable and disease-resistant, upright bush. For an abundance of flowers, prune to half its size each year. ZONES 5–10

'The Mayflower'

### Teasing Georgia

A yellow rose with a refined air and a robust constitution. Cups of deep golden yellow quilled and quartered petals are prettily framed by pale outer petals. Good repeat blooms on a healthy and vigorous but graceful bush which can be encouraged to climb. A multiple award winner. ZONES 4–9

### The Countryman

fragrant

A big, handsome ruffle of a rose with quilled petals of clear, deep pink, it resembles its ancestor 'Comte de Chambord' in color, long pointed leaves and delectable perfume (some say wild strawberries mixed with old rose). But it has a more spreading, arching habit of growth. Disease-resistant and reliable, but remember to deadhead. ZONES 4–9

### The Dark Lady

fragrant

Full-petaled, double ruffled blooms are deep rich red, well displayed against dark green foliage, and have a particularly charming quality, hard to pinpoint. The breeder compares them to Chinese tree peonies depicted on old fabrics and wallpapers. Habit of growth is upright and moderate. ZONES 4–9

### The Herbalist

This is a remarkable rose. For the last six years I have grown it in a stony field at the ends of rows of grape vines – purely for its decorative effect. Except for its first season, it has never been watered, it is fed sparingly but mulched heavily – and it is totally glorious. The rose was named for its resemblance to *R. gallica officinalis*, often called 'The Apothecary's Rose' because it was used to make medicinal lotions, potions and powders in the Middle Ages.

'The Herbalist' is considerably larger but has the same semi-double form and dark glowing pink – almost carmine – petals that open out to accentuate bright yellow stamens. The upright bush is reliably robust and hardy and can reach 6 ½ ft. (2 m) unless

Top: 'Sweet Juliet'
Above: 'The Herbalist'

Top: 'The Dark Lady'
Above: 'Teasing Georgia'

you prune to keep it smaller. In my garden there are few roses that flower as long and as generously and attract as much attention as 'The Herbalist' – which is not surprising considering it is a direct descendant of the old Bourbon rose, 'Louise Odier', a model of perfection in every way. ZONES 4–9

## The Mayflower

A recently introduced rose that represents an important breakthrough in English roses – or almost any roses for that matter. 'The Mayflower' is said to be completely resistant to black spot, powdery mildew and rust! (Now, if nothing would eat it, that would be perfection indeed – and far too much to hope.) Deep rose pink, full-petaled flowers, opening

flat, appear with regularity from spring through fall. Habit of growth is twiggy but bushy and the foliage is small but plentiful. The rose was named to mark the launching of David Austin's American catalog and the opening of the David Austin Rose Garden at Matterhorn Nurseries north of New York City. ZONES 4–9

## The Pilgrim

Clear yellow flowers open to large flat circles with many small inner petals and larger outer petals all precisely arranged in layers. It's an upright, free-flowering shrubby bush and one of the strongest, healthiest and most reliable of English roses – a good garden rose. ZONES 4–9

Top: 'Winchester Cathedral'
Above: 'Wenlock'

## The Prince

fragrant

Lovers of black-red velvet roses, read on. To heck with simplicity and elegance – what I really fall for is the undiluted over-the-top opulence of 'The Prince'. Here is a rose fully double, cupped and quartered, combining the sumptuousness of the Bourbons with the plush, purple velvet richness of the Gallicas – a dusty deepest crimson overlaid with purple. Outer petals roll back curl upon curl, not in the least like gauzy butterflies wings, but as heavy and substantial as folds of satin. But there is a price to pay. Blooms will burn in the hot sun and stems are weak. The plant itself is not robust and will need tender loving care. At least it will never get too big. ZONES 4–9

## Wenlock

fragrant

Red roses in general tend to be poor growers and those that do grow well lack fragrance. 'Wenlock' is an exception – a big bright crimson rose with a heavenly scent and a strong constitution. The bush is of moderate height with large, handsome, disease-resistant foliage. Flowers are freely produced. What more could you want? ZONES 5–10

## William Morris

fragrant

A rose of many virtues. Big rosettes of flowers are a lovely luminous combination of apricot and pink and freely borne. The bush is tall, hardy and disease-resistant. An altogether pleasing shrub that can also be used as a moderate climber. ZONES 4–10

## William Shakespeare 2000

very fragrant

I grew 'William Shakespeare 1987', which was a beautiful rose with a weak constitution. The new 2000 model combines beauty of flower form with excellent disease-resistance. Superb, velvety crimson flowers tinged with rich purple as they age, are full-petaled, cupped and quartered. Habit of growth is neat and upright. The breeder believes it to be his best crimson rose to date. Get it! ZONES 5–10

## Winchester Cathedral

A white sport of 'Mary Rose' with all of its parent's virtues. Glistening white, loosely double flowers with amber stamens are freely borne on a moderate, well-foliaged, disease-resistant bush. Occasionally you might find a pink rose among the white but the plant is so pretty and well behaved that you will excuse this small indiscretion. ZONES 5–9

## Windrush

A stylish rose and one of my favorites. Very large and semi-single, the form is a departure from the incurving cups and many-petaled rosettes so often

Above: 'Windrush' in an informal corner of the garden.
Right: 'Windrush'

seen in English roses. Ten to 15 wavy, lemon-cream petals surround long, light yellow stamens. Tips of the stamens darken and petals pale to milky opal as the flower ages. The shrub is big, bold and vigorous, sending out long canes that can be trained along a fence or trellis. Remember to deadhead. It flowers prolifically in spring and early summer, followed by large hips which must be removed if you want a second flush of flowers. ZONES 5–9

CHAPTER 5

# *Cultivation*

"I consider everything hardy until I've killed it myself." I don't know who said that but I like it. Roses are easy to grow. Like most living things, they need food, water, sun and shelter. A measure of love is always advantageous. A bewildering amount of literature has been written on the subject of rose cultivation, a lot of it contradictory. Too much perplexing advice takes the pleasure out of anything and, surely when it comes to growing roses, pleasure is what it's all about. If your way of growing roses is different from mine and it works for you, stay with it. Our gardens are a reflection of our personalities but tempered by our creativity, energy, finances, spare time … We are all limited in one way or another and there's more than a little magic in gardening.

'Belle Story'

## Choosing your roses

It is desirable to see a rose growing before you buy it. Visit display gardens at nurseries; check with gardening friends and your nearest botanical gardens. You will then have a much better idea of the plant as a whole – blooms, perfume, foliage, habit of growth – and its possibilities in your garden. Spring/early summer is the best time to see most roses in their prime but flowering times will vary with the location and the weather. Or you can take a risk and have the thrill of ordering from a catalog and waiting.

### *Bare root plants*

Some nurseries specialize in bare root plants which are usually ordered from a catalog and delivered

in fall or early winter. They are often cheaper and smaller than container-grown plants but they quickly catch up because they have time to establish themselves before they flower.

Plants will arrive freshly dug from the nursery fields, packed in a box with their roots in a damp medium – straw, sawdust, peat moss or shredded paper – and wrapped in plastic. A strong plant will have a thick rootstock and three or more substantial shoots coming from the bud union, although some old roses may have only two. A plant with one shoot is unacceptable. Roots should be numerous and a reasonable length. Take care not to let them dry out. Soak them in a bucket of water for a few hours if you like. If you cannot plant them immediately, dig a small trench anywhere in the garden where the soil is suitable and "heel" them in. This means

Opposite: Hybrid musk 'Cornelia' flowering prolifically.

placing the plants in the trench, covering the roots with earth and pressing down firmly with your feet. As long as they are kept moist, they can stay like this for weeks – or months – if necessary.

### Container-grown plants

These are sold in pots and bags by nurseries and garden centers. Be wary of small plants in small pots. Look for strong growth rather than flowers.

## Planting

I know this is a lot to ask but try not to buy a plant on impulse, and then walk around the garden looking for a place to fit it in. A bit of planning can be the difference between triumph and disaster. Planting position is crucial. Although there are a few roses that cope with shade, the majority need sun for at least half the day. An open position with not too much competition at the roots but shelter from strong winds is ideal. If other plants are too close to your new rose, they will take advantage of

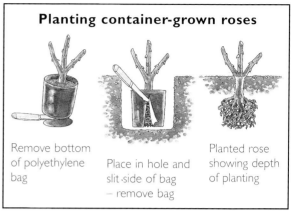

**Planting container-grown roses**

Remove bottom of polyethylene bag

Place in hole and slit side of bag – remove bag

Planted rose showing depth of planting

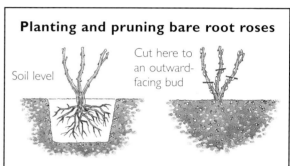

**Planting and pruning bare root roses**

Soil level

Cut here to an outward-facing bud

Check the size and depth of the hole before planting.

The hole needs to be deep enough to cover the bud union with about 3 in. (7 cm) of soil.

the nutrients you have prepared for it and constant strong winds can break it at the base or loosen its hold on the soil. Your small plant will become a big one – possibly a very big one – and will need air space, so consider carefully where you choose to plant it.

It is unprofitable to plant a rose in heavy, water-logged soil. You can improve it by drainage and the addition of peat moss. On the other hand, if your soil is almost pure sand, you will need to add organic matter. In any soil type, *humus* is the operative word when it comes to growing roses well. Ideally, you should incorporate a generous amount of compost or well-rotted manure deeply into the soil. Fresh manure will burn the roots. The words *well-rotted* should be engraved on every gardener's heart.

Dig a hole bigger than you think you will need. It should be wide enough to accommodate the out-spread roots of the rose and deep enough to cover the bud union (where the branches meet) with about 3 in. (7 cm) of soil. Opinions vary on depth of planting. Deep planting prevents wind rock, encourages shoots from the base and prevents frost damage to tender young shoots.

### Bare root roses

Make a little mound of potting mix at the bottom of the hole so that the rose sits comfortably with roots spread out, then half fill the hole with enriched soil or good quality potting mix. Water well to settle the soil. Fill the hole.

### Container-grown roses

If the plant is in a plastic bag, place the bag in the hole, then slit the side, disturbing the roots as little as possible. If in a plastic pot, place the pot in the hole, tilt and remove plant and soil in one block. Continue planting as for bare root roses.

When planting is completed, gently fork in half a handful each of bone meal and blood meal. Firm the soil around the roses gently with your foot or hands and water well, making sure the water penetrates down to the roots of the rose.

*R. dupontii* covering a rustic trellis.

Unless the rose is a climber, prune to approximately 6 in. (15 cm) from ground level, just above an outward-facing bud. This allows the plant to direct its energy into growing new roots rather than maintaining leaves – and growth will be bushy rather than leggy.

Put a substantial, indelibly marked label beside the plant. (Yes, I know you think you will remember its name, but the odds are against it.)

### Climbers

Try not to plant climbers any closer than 20 in. (50 cm) away from a wall. If the roots are all on one side, plant with the roots running away from the wall and position the plant so that it leans slightly towards the wall.

When planting a rose to climb a tree, it is often better to plant close to the trunk rather than some distance away where the tree roots are greediest. Dig out a pocket where you intend to plant, preferably on the sunny side, and fill it with soil or potting mix. Take care to water the rose well over the next few months. Tree branches may shield it from rain and it will have to compete with tree roots. Bear in mind that the rose will tend to flower on the sunny side of the tree.

### Standards

Drive a strong supporting stake into the center of the hole, then plant the rose in the normal way. The bud union is up in the air so you need to look for the mark on the stem to see how deep it was planted in the nursery. This should be level with the soil after planting. Tie the rose to the stake near the base and just below the branches.

## Roses in containers

Roses, including climbers, can grow well in containers but it is essential that the container is big enough and the rose is fed and watered consistently. I wouldn't plant a rose in a pot less than 20 in. (50 cm) in diameter and 16 in. (40 cm) deep. Make sure there are drainage holes in the base. Place broken pieces of brick, terra-cotta or stones in the bottom and cover with a layer of damp peat to stop soil from blocking the holes, then fill with good quality potting soil. (You get what you pay for.) Plant in the normal way. Deep watering is essential. A coffee cupful now and then won't do a thing. The roots must never be allowed to dry out. Renew the top 4–6 in. (10–15 cm) of soil each year and, unless your container is huge, cut the rose back and re-pot it every third year.

## Transplanting

Even a large established rose can be successfully transplanted. Moving a plant in its dormant period is advisable: early spring or late fall in cool climates; through winter in more temperate zones. Prune the rose hard – by about two thirds – and water well for three days before you dig it out as carefully as possible. It may be impossible to dig out a well-established old rose without considerable root damage. This doesn't matter too much. Trim long, tangled, fibrous roots and plant in the normal way. Keep it well watered and protected from hot sunlight for a few weeks if you can. Don't panic if it loses its leaves.

## Feeding

Old roses are obviously survivors and will grow in

An elegant combination of urns and old roses.

any reasonable soil. If you want them to grow and flower well, it pays to feed them. Repeat-flowering roses of any variety need regular feeding. Roses love humus and a soil rich in organic matter will result in healthy plants that bloom generously. The best way to achieve this is to fork in compost, bone meal, blood meal (blood and bone) and composted manures. A mixture of blood meal and bone meal is particularly good. It smells foul and the dog will love it, but water it in and it will disappear quite quickly. You don't have to collect manure fresh from the fields and wait until it rots. Well-rotted manures can usually be bought in large and small quantities.

If you don't already have a compost bin, consider getting one, no matter how small your garden or high-tech your kitchen. All household waste except meat, fat and dairy products can go in it and you can give back to the soil a measure of what you take out. If you have access to seaweed, it makes an excellent organic manure.

A combination of commercial rose fertilizer and composted manures is ideal. Fertilizers specifically prepared for roses contain the correct proportions of nitrogen, phosphorus and potassium, plus trace elements such as iron, zinc, boron, etc., necessary for growth. Follow the maker's instructions and don't be tempted to overfeed. And most importantly, water the fertilizer into the soil. Fertilizer sitting on top of dry soil is doing nothing and putting fertilizer into dry soil can burn plant roots.

Give the roses two main feeds – in early spring and after the first flush of bloom is finished. It is often convenient to give the roses their spring feed immediately after pruning.

Liquid seaweed and fish emulsion are excellent, but unless you live by the sea and make your own, they are an expensive option. I like to use them as a tonic foliage spray whenever I think of it through summer. Don't waste banana skins – put them around your roses. They disappear quickly and provide the roses with calcium, magnesium, sulfur, phosphates, sodium and silica – minute quantities of course but that's all they need.

## Watering
This will depend on your climate. Roses are deep rooted and cope better than we imagine during a long dry period. However, dry roots stress the plant and a stressed plant is open to diseases and excessive winter die-back.

A casual sprinkle every day only encourages fibrous roots towards the surface which does more harm than good. Ideally, they need a good soaking once or twice a week, preferably in the early morning so that foliage dries quickly. Wet leaves encourage fungus diseases. A trickle irrigation system which conserves water but can be left on long enough to deliver water to the roots is excellent.

## Mulching
Mulch, mulch mulch! Mulches can feed the plants, suppress weeds and provide a protective blanket for the roots. Put your roses to bed in late fall under a thick mulch of straw, composted bark, pine needles, grape marc, rice hulls, old carpet, jute sacking, coconut fiber, cardboard, newspapers – or whatever is available in your area. Almost anything that gradually decomposes is fine.

After the early spring feed, mulch with compost and/or manures if you can and top with a summer mulch that will retain moisture, reduce soil temperatures and, at the same time, look attractive in the garden – composted bark for example. A thin layer of grass clippings is fine but make sure the grass has not been sprayed. Roses are particularly susceptible to weedkillers.

## Deadheading
For continuity of flower in repeat-flowering roses, it is important to deadhead.

If you remove a spent flower before hips begin to form, new flowers will be produced. The plant will continue to produce seed and, in the process, it will flower again.

You can simply snap off the flower head below the abscission layer (a swollen section in the stem just below the flower) or cut the stem just above the first bud-eye above a five-leafed branchlet.

## Suckers
Sometimes the rootstock of a rose sends out suckers which are recognizable because they come from below ground level and their foliage is different from that of the grafted rose. These must be removed promptly. Scrape away a little soil if necessary, find where the sucker joins the root and pull it off as cleanly as possible.

## Cuttings
Although there are nurseries specializing in cutting-grown roses, most commercially grown roses are

propagated by a process called *budding* which involves taking a growth bud from the required rose and inserting in the stem of a strong-growing *stock* rose. For the home gardener, growing roses from cuttings is a satisfying way of acquiring new roses.

In temperate regions, hardwood cuttings taken in early fall have a good chance of success. Old roses, climbers and ramblers strike more readily than Hybrid Teas and Floribundas, but don't let that discourage you. Take more cuttings than you need on the basis that about half of them will grow. Choose a healthy branch that has flowered during the current season. Cuttings should be severed at a joint or taken from the mid-section of the branch, contain three or four growth buds and be approximately the length and diameter of a pencil. Thinner cuttings from naturally twiggy roses are fine as long as they have sufficient growth nodes.

Take care not to let the cuttings dry out. If you have access to willow trees, chop up a few leaves and the whippy ends of young branches, put them in a jar, cover with warm water and stand your cuttings in this willow tea overnight. This seems to work for me. Willows contain salicylic acid, but so do aspirin. One aspirin in a jar of water would be as beneficial.

Remove all the leaves or let the top two remain – opinions differ. Immediately before planting, re-cut the base at a 45° angle just below a growth bud using sharp pruning shears (secateurs). At this point you can dip it in rooting hormone if you haven't used willow water but check the sell-by date.

Cuttings can go in a container or the open ground. In cold regions, follow the same process in midsummer.

### Container method

Fill a container with sharp sand or perlite mixed with a little potting soil. Water well and let drain. Insert the cuttings (several in one pot are fine) so that at least two growth buds apart from the base are under the soil – usually about two thirds of the whole. Use a pencil to begin the holes so that the bases of the

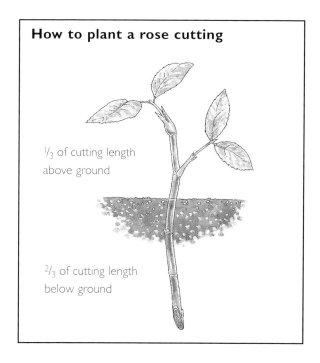

**How to plant a rose cutting**

¹/₃ of cutting length above ground

²/₃ of cutting length below ground

cuttings are not damaged. Water again and place in dappled shade. Make sure the mix in the container doesn't dry out but don't overwater. You can make a little greenhouse with a plastic bag secured with an elastic band over the top if you like.

### Open ground

Dig a little trench in the vegetable garden or a similar suitable spot, put a layer of sand or perlite at the bottom, insert your cuttings, infill the trench so the cuttings are held firmly and water. The lucky survivors can be re-sited in about six months but it is better to leave them until the following fall.

## Protection from cold

Protection from winter cold is important but very difficult to state categorically. While a simple answer would be nice, there really isn't one. The majority of roses will tolerate zone 4 winter minimum temperatures, but roses grown in zones 4 and 5 will need some winter protection. As important as the zone is the type of winter you experience, e.g., a wet winter, very cold, dry winter, how long snow lies on the ground (these can all vary considerably even within the same hardiness zone). Also important is the class of rose you want to grow.

In zones 4–5, if snow cover is reliable and deep, the hardier roses will be protected by this natural insulation below the snow line. However, where winters are dry, e.g., Colorado, protection may then be needed, even for some of the hardier types, to avoid die-back to the ground. Teas, Noisettes, Portlands, Chinas and many Hybrid Teas always need protection below zone 6, regardless of snow cover.

Winter hardiness in any particular variety of rose can depend on a number of variables, including the way the plant has been fertilized, the weather during fall, the amount of snow and the micro-climate the plant grows in. Roses can be winter hardy but spring tender. When freeze and thaw alternate and tender growth is too early, the roses become vulnerable to damage. In particularly cold areas, roses can be protected during winter in a variety of ways. The simplest are mounding with earth or covering with a wood chip mulch to a depth of about 6 in (15 cm). Wrapping the plants in sacking or using rose cones are other options.

Roses bred from the following species are considered to be the most cold hardy: *R. alba, R. centifolia, R. foetida, R. gallica, R. rugosa, R. spinosissima.* Teas, Hybrid Teas, Hybrid Perpetuals and Noisettes are not generally hardy (there are exceptions) in extreme cold but most roses are cold hardy to zone 4, with winter protection.

## Pruning

*A person who calls a rose by any other name has probably just been pruning.*

A<small>NON</small>

The main canes of all roses begin to lose their vigor eventually. Keep a check on this and every few years cut out one or two canes. There is no great universal law that states roses must be pruned annually. Some need it, some don't. We prune to remove dead wood and encourage the natural process of renewal – and

to keep a rose a manageable size. A rule of thumb says that the closer a rose is to a species, the lighter the pruning; the closer to a modern rose, the harder the pruning, However, like most aspects of pruning, that rule can be debated. When you prune is more important than how you prune.

There are only two rules:

1. Prune once-flowering roses as soon as possible after flowering is finished – i.e., summer prune. They flower on the previous season's growth and if you prune in winter, you will lose potential flowers. Summer pruned, they will grow fresh new leaves and look handsome even without flowers.
2. Prune repeat-flowering roses just before new growth begins – i.e., late winter, depending on your climate.

However, David Austin recommends that his roses be pruned in the period of maximum dormancy on the basis that later pruning will cut off significantly sized new shoots which will encourage the production of soft new shoots more likely to be damaged by late frosts than those that have grown slowly in cold weather.

The traditional method of pruning roses is to use sharp pruning shears (secateurs) to make a cut at a 45° angle just above an outward-facing growth bud. However, for pruning shrub roses, the latest word

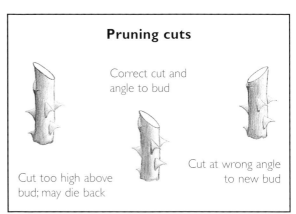

**Pruning cuts**

Correct cut and angle to bud

Cut too high above bud; may die back

Cut at wrong angle to new bud

is that shears are out and hedge trimmers, which leave more leafy, twiggy growth on the rose, are in. The reasoning is that more leaves mean more photosynthesis which means more flowers. The choice is yours.

### Pruning old roses

One of the nice things about old roses is that you do not prune them to a few pathetic sticks in winter. Apart from planting time, most old, shrub roses are better not pruned for the first two or three years to give them time to build a structure. You may then decide to leave them largely unpruned apart from the removal of dead and diseased wood, spindly shoots and those that are crossed or tangled.

### Pruning English roses

Again, there is no rule that says you must prune, but most benefit from regular pruning. Removing a third is regarded as light pruning, two thirds as hard pruning.

### Pruning hedges

If you are planting a rose hedge, prune the plants hard in their first year to encourage bushy growth at the base.

### Pruning climbers

Initially the emphasis is on training. Bend strong young canes to fan out from the base so that they are as near horizontal as possible. This causes the plant to send up flowering shoots all along the canes instead of just at the top. Elbow to hand is a rough guide for spacing between horizontal canes. Pruning consists of shortening the flowering side shoot to three or four growth buds each year and removing old unprofitable canes from the base as the plant matures. To encourage new shoots to grow from the base, make a small cut in the bark just above a dormant growth bud.

### Pruning ramblers

Prune them as climbers if you wish – i.e., shorten the side shoots each year and be rigorous in the removal of main canes. Failure to do this means that next year's growth will be from the ends of side shoots and after a few years of this you will have thinner growth and a lot of non-flowering wood. Or if you have the

David Austin's 'Mary Rose' pruned as a standard lines a formal walk.

space, you can wait until you are faced with a huge rampant old rambler and attack it then.

### Pruning standards

Prune in the same way as a bush rose, concentrating on keeping a symmetrical shape.

Remove all prunings and be sure to dispose of them.

## Pests and diseases

> *Roses have thorns, and silver*
>  *Fountains mud;*
> *Cloud and eclipses stain both moon and sun,*
> *And loathsome canker lives in sweetest bud.*
> *All men make faults.*
>
> ANON

Too much is written about diseases in roses. Unless you have a special dispensation from God, most of your roses will get black spot and some of them will mildew. There is no point in railing against it. These little problems are a fact of life but they can be alleviated to a certain degree and they rarely kill a rose. Most times, the roses can cope with mildew if you can put up with the slight unsightliness.

It has been said that the best fertilizer is the footsteps of the gardener and the same can be said about the prevention of diseases and, to some extent, the control of pests. The old-fashioned term *good-husbandry*, which simply means looking at your plants and supplying their needs, is the best defence. Strong, well-cared-for roses will resist diseases or throw them off without coming to much harm.

However, some roses are disease prone. We persevere with them because their flowers are just so beautiful. The trouble is that they can infect other roses, so sensibly they should be "shovel pruned," in other words dug out and disposed of. To be ruthless is a handy attribute in gardening as in life. Ideally, we should fall in love with roses that are breathtakingly beautiful, heavily fragrant and disease-resistant. A bit like falling in love with handsome, kind, rich men, I suppose.

### Spraying

The decision to use chemical or organic sprays – or no sprays at all – depends on your gardening philosophy.

*Spring and summer:* a variety of commercial sprays are available which control both fungal diseases and insect predators. Newer and more environmentally friendly sprays appear each year. Consult your local nursery for the remedy best suited to your problem. Follow the instructions and spray regularly. Intermittent spraying seems to do more harm than good, rather like not finishing a course of antibiotics. The best time to spray is in the evening when you are less likely to harm useful insects and spray will be more easily absorbed during the night.

*Winter:* a clean-up spraying program to destroy overwintering spores of fungal diseases, scale and eggs of aphids and mites is important because it means you can greet spring with healthy roses.

1. *Optional* – at the beginning of winter, spray with lime sulfur. It defoliates the plants and ensures they are dormant throughout winter. Drench bushes and surrounding soil. Rake up and discard old leaves. Do not mix with any other spray and do not use any other spray for three weeks. I use lime sulfur when roses have been badly infected the previous year. It smells horrible and discolors paintwork.
2. *Recommended* – a copper-based spray (copper oxychloride or copper hydroxide) combined with horticultural oil at winter strength. Follow the manufacturer's instructions on the product label. Use this spray twice if possible before spring shoots emerge, leaving a two-week interval between applications.

### Pests

Gardening lore says if you see something on your roses that isn't moving, kill it. If it is moving, leave

Top: The bane of all rose growers – aphids.
Above: Black spot is the most common disease of roses.

it because it's probably going to kill something. Mixed planting, rather than a monoculture, can reduce the number of pests. Nectar-rich species such as dianthus, daisies, sage, catmint, etc., attract beneficial insects which feast on them. Birds are a tremendous help, especially when they have young to feed. It's a good idea to encourage small birds near your roses by feeding them – but not too much.

There will be times, however, depending on where you live, when hungry hordes of predators will descend and there is not all that much you can do about it. It will pass – that's life.

When it comes to four-legged pests – deer, rabbits, possums – your guess is as good as mine. To the best of my knowledge, they do not relish rugosas.

*Aphids* (Greenfly): these appear in spring in their thousands to suck the life out of roses. Get all the help you can – plant honesty (*Lunaria annua*) and *Phacelia* spp. to attract the hover fly which eats them. If you don't have too many plants, there's always digit control which means stripping them off and scrunching them with your fingers. Grandmother's method of knocking them down with a high pressure hose is surprisingly effective but needs to be done regularly.

Another simple method which seems to reduce the population is spraying with liquid fish or seaweed fertilizer. If none of those methods appeals, use an insecticide which does not harm friendly insects. But do something because aphids seriously weaken roses.

*Red spider mites:* a problem in warm dry areas. Barely visible to the naked eye, it is often some time before you realize they are there. Foliage becomes pale and eventually falls off. Look closely at the underside of the leaves to detect a tracery of webbing. Most insecticides won't kill them because they are spiders, not insects.

Wetting the leaves every morning – by hand or irrigation spray – will inhibit the infestation. Or you can use a miticide.

*White scale:* most often seen on mature wood, especially old climbers. These pests should be killed by the winter spraying program. However, the pest has a flying stage and can spread to other roses. Use horticultural oil at summer strength.

*Caterpillars:* sawfly larvae (rose slug) which eat the surface of leaves creating a lace curtain effect can

Roses stressed by lack of water can be especially susceptible to powdery mildew.

be controlled by hand picking or spraying with an insecticide. The leaf-rolling sawfly is more likely to attack roses in the shade and can be best controlled by removing the rolled-up leaves.

*Japanese beetles:* these can be a scourge, particularly in the eastern states. Adults are about half an inch (1 cm) long with metallic blue-green bodies and can quickly strip flowers and foliage. Larvae are half to one inch (1–3 cm) long and gray-white. Having devoured everything in sight, they disappear until next summer. The larval grub lives in soil under turf grass and so lack of lawns would discourage them – but the neighbors would have to cooperate. Hand picking the adult beetles into a bucket of soapy water in the early mornings is the safest option. Insecticides are reputed to be ineffectual. Check with your garden center.

*Curculio weevils:* these hatch in late spring and continue through summer. Mostly, they drill holes and lay eggs in rose buds which promptly die, but they will also eat foliage. Meticulous deadheading and hand picking every morning decreases the population but it's not a practical option if you have a large number of roses.

## Diseases

*Black spot:* this is the most common affliction – almost a fact of rose life – so don't panic. Black spots appear on leaves which turn yellow and fall. If you plan to spray with a fungicide, treatment must begin early in summer before disease symptoms appear because nothing will eradicate black spot once it has taken hold. Picking off the infected leaves into a bag at an early stage and disposing of them is helpful and may prevent black spot from spreading to other roses, but try not to end up with completely skeletal bushes.

If you choose not to use a chemical spray, you might like to try a mixture of skim milk and water, half and half. In tests a few years ago it was reported to be "at least as effective as chemical sprays" – which may not mean a lot. However, you would expect the lactic acid in the milk to create conditions inhospitable for fungi.

*Powdery mildew:* young leaves and buds are covered with grayish white powdery patches. Roses under stress, especially during a dry season, are particularly susceptible.

Some roses will mildew no matter what you do for them and if you find it too unsightly, they are better culled. However many roses, too beautiful to lose, will mildew and then throw it off as if it had been a bad cold. A spray of 1 teaspoon (5 ml) of baking soda and a few drops of liquid soap in 8 cups (2 L) of water every 10 days is worth trying before you resort to a fungicide.

*Rust:* this debilitating disease is usually first noticed when obvious orange spots appear on the underside of leaves, although the first sign of infection is a few isolated spots on both sides. Remove infected leaves and dispose of them. Spray with a fungicide. It is important to treat this disease because overwintering spores are quick to infect the plant next season. Some roses are susceptible but, as in the case of mildew, they are quite capable of throwing off an attack and growing fresh green leaves.

# CHAPTER 6

# Landscaping with Old Roses

*"I go around other people's gardens with a jealous eye. I see someone's roses growing without a touch of blackspot ... and I feel sick with envy. What makes me a really happy woman is to go around some garden I think wrongly constructed, planted in bad taste and rather untidy. I am then extraordinarily civil to the owner, saying how beautiful everything is and go home in a highly contented frame of mind ... It is easy, if you have a modicum of taste, to create a pretty garden, but it is damn difficult to keep it going."*

LADY CAROLINE SOMERSET, *THE ENGLISHWOMAN'S GARDEN*

What other genus of plants could be used for so many landscaping purposes as the rose? We could plan an entire garden using nothing but roses and a few structures. There are roses to suit every garden – English, Mediterranean, romantic, minimalist, formal, informal, seashore, hillside, wild and whatever else you can think of.

## Fragrance

This is an important consideration, particularly when planting near windows, doors, paths and parts of the garden used for outdoor living.

Of all the senses, smell is the most complex. Unlike sight and sound, it cannot be recalled in absence, yet it evokes lost memories intensely. However beautiful a garden may be, without fragrance it doesn't touch the heart and almost any sort of garden can put us in the mood to consider it beautiful if the air is full of delectable perfumes.

Most roses are perfumed but the roses listed as fragrant in this book are noticeably scented – at least to me. The appreciation of perfume is very much a personal thing – and also dependent on the time of day and the weather. Roses are said to smell their best on warm dry mornings. The makers of attar,

Opposite: 'Cecile Brunner' as a backdrop to a garden pond.

the oil which contains the scent, have known for centuries that roses must be picked between 4:30 and 9:30 in the morning. Having said that, I'm sure my roses are their most fragrant on warm still evenings, particularly if they are in an enclosed garden. The correct way to smell a rose is to cup your hands around it, breathe gently and sniff.

Some roses hold their perfume within their petals but others waft it into the air around them, an admirable virtue in hedging roses. I have a small hedge of the Rugosa 'Hansa' planted on a driveway entrance which never fails to put guests in a good mood. The same can be said for Alba Semi-plena along a road frontage.

## Companions in borders and beds

Grand beds and borders filled with a mix of roses, shrubs and perennials are impressive but labor intensive so it is wise to keep them to a manageable size. Fill them to the brim and mulch heavily so there is little opportunity for weeds. Enjoy them through spring and summer, then give them a massive cleanup in late fall and put them to bed under a winter mulch. As long as roses are fed well, they perform happily in the company of shrubs and non-invasive plants. Garden centers carry a wide selection of suitable annuals and perennials. The choice is yours.

The yellow 'Charles Austin', along with perennial companion plants, makes a spectacular garden border.

When it comes to edgings, varieties of boxwood (*Buxus* spp.) have been a traditional formal edging since Roman times, but try anything that takes your fancy and can be clipped to shape – dwarf varieties of wine dark barberry (*Berberis* spp.) for example. For a more informal look there is always lavender, mauve-blue catmint (*Nepeta* x *faassenii*) or clumps of lady's mantle (*Alchemilla mollis*) with chartreuse flowers and big frilled velvet leaves.

Have fun with color combinations. Gardening is painting with a very broad brush with the advantage that if it doesn't quite work out, you can rearrange it all next year. The verb *to move* is essential in any gardener's vocabulary.

## Roses as shrubs

Many roses make excellent specimen shrubs. Some of the once-flowering old roses, particularly substantial Albas and Gallicas, make impressive shrubs and are a delight in the spring garden. However, repeat-flowering roses are preferable in an area where you want summer flowers. Hybrid Musks are excellent for this purpose. English roses that lend themselves to this treatment include 'Graham Thomas', 'Leander', 'Abraham Darby', 'Windrush', 'Charles Austin', 'A Shropshire Lad', 'William Morris', 'Teasing Georgia', and 'Gertrude Jekyll'. 'Dapple Dawn' and 'Redcoat' make big sprawling shrubs.

Vigorous shrub roses may need structures to support them. If they are planted in a lawn, make sure sufficient space is left for the application of fertilizers. Roses grown in grass, rather than in rich bedding soil, need all the help they can get if they are to flower continuously, so it pays to feed them well. Foliage feed occasionally and use a long-term, slow-acting fertilizer to supplement their regular feeding program. Make several (depending on the size of the plant) deep little holes with a pencil around the drip line and drop a teaspoonful (5 ml) of granules in each.

*Pegging down*: if you have the space, the time and the inclination, this technique can be used to spectacular effect with lax roses with long pliable canes. New shoots are pruned when they reach about 5 ft. (1.5 m) and then pegged down in a horizontal position to encourage each shoot to flower along its entire length. Select the longest shoot first, remove approximately 18 in. (45 cm) of growth from the tip, then peg into a horizontal position making sure that the cane is still some distance from the ground. This should be done with black string attached to the cane and to wire hooks which are pushed into the soil. Repeat this procedure with all the longest growths to develop a mushroom pattern. Cut a few short canes to bloom in the center.

## Standard roses

Tall, medium and patio standards are available to add height to a flat garden as well as a touch of formality. They also save space in a small garden and allow for a variety of interesting little plants underneath them. Weeping standards are romantic and formal at the same time.

## Roses in a woodland garden

Hardy, disease-resistant, easy-care species rugosas and ramblers can light up woodland areas with flowers and interesting foliage in summer and leaf color and bright hips in fall. Trees make wonderful supports for cascading ramblers.

## Climbers

You don't need much land to garden vertically. If there is a house, there will be walls and fences to cover with roses. If you are concerned about accessibility for repainting, you can train the roses on a trellis which hangs from hooks on the wall. When

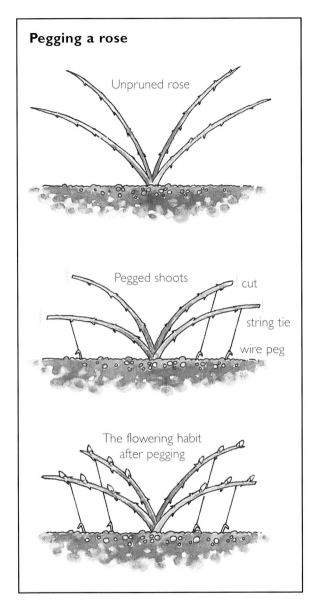

**Pegging a rose**

Unpruned rose

Pegged shoots — cut / string tie / wire peg

The flowering habit after pegging

you need to repaint, unhook the trellis and lay it flat on the ground with the roses attached. You could do the same with a frame around wires. Alternatively you can use lengths of plastic-coated expanding wire hooked to the base of the wall and up under the eaves. Or you can simply prune the roses hard.

Summerhouses, verandas, porches, pergolas, pillars, arbors and arches are all improved with roses. A flat garden is almost always a boring garden. Give it height and interest with a pergola walk, an arbor tucked against a fence line or a series of arches over paths – and make it beautiful by covering these structures with climbing roses. A simple post wrapped around with wire mesh will support a pillar rose.

Climbing roses combine happily with other climbers if they are not too rampant. Clematis are the perfect companions. Summer-flowering hybrids of *Clematis taxensis*, *C. jackmanii* and *C. viticella* are ideal, especially with once-flowering roses because they will continue flowering when the rose has finished. Choose colors to complement or contrast. As clematis like their roots in the shade, it is best to plant them on the shady side of an established rose. Plant a vigorous, repeat-flowering, climbing rose with wisteria to provide flowers when the wisteria has finished its spring blooming.

## Roses as hedges

Most gardens can be improved with hedges even if the hedge consists of only four or five roses dividing one part of the garden from another. Roses make superb, floriferous hedges. Almost any roses can be used but most of us choose repeat-flowering, well-foliaged, shrub roses with a dense bushy habit of growth. The hardy Rugosas will give you an interesting hedge for most of the year with flowers, foliage and hips. Many of the Hybrid Musks make substantial, strong-growing hedges and you can prune them to the size you want. Ramblers can make huge, gloriously informal hedges if you have the space. If you want an impenetrable barrier along a boundary, plant the viciously thorned 'Mermaid' (zone 7), evergreen in warm climates. It is capable of flowering all year and even a few blooms in winter are enough to delight.

## Roses as groundcovers

Roses are not true groundcovers and will not suppress weeds as effectively as creeping plants and prostrate shrubs, but low growing roses with a spreading habit can cover terraces, banks and low walls very prettily. They can be cut back when required and never become invasive. Moderate ramblers – e.g., 'May Queen' – can be kept low to the ground. 'Max Graf' is a Rugosa hybrid with prostrate growth habits and trailing shoots that will take root. The low growing species rose, *R. nitida*, grown on its own roots, will sucker freely and cover large areas with glossy serrated foliage that colors in fall and big single rich pink flowers followed by bright red hips.

The Hybrid Musk 'Ballerina' will form spreading mounds if pruned to shape.

Left: The climbing Tea 'Gloire de Dijon'
Opposite: Old roses as shrubs, climbers and ramblers create a charming cottage garden atmosphere.

# CHAPTER 7

# Decadent Diversions

*Gather ye rosebuds while ye may*
*Partaking of all pleasure,*
*We only know our fate today,*
*Cannot the future measure.*

ROBERT HERRICK

## Microwaving rose petals

This is an instant drying method for potpourri that ensures there will be no bugs.

Microwave about five roses at a time, face down on a paper towel, for approximately 1½ minutes, depending on the strength of your microwave.

## Rose oil

This recipe was given to me in Kashmir. Pour 2 cups (500 ml) of olive oil into a wide-necked glass jar and add as many fragrant rose petals as possible, pressing them down in the oil. Leave in the sun – a window-sill is fine – for six days, then strain, pressing the oil out of the petals. Repeat the process using fresh petals six times until the oil smells strongly of roses. Store in airtight bottles and use sparingly to perfume potpourri or in fruit salads, etc.

### Rose Petal Conserve

(A nice chunky conserve.)

4 cups (1 L) rose petals (dark are best)
3 cups (³/4 L) water
3 cups (³/4 L) sugar
2 tablespoons (15 ml) lemon juice

Above and opposite: Color-themed bouquets of David Austin and old-fashioned roses.

Rinse petals, remove pale "heels" at base, then layer petals in a bowl with sugar between each layer. Cover and leave overnight. Put petals, sugar, water and lemon juice in a saucepan and bring gently to a boil. Simmer till setting point – although it will not set hard – pour into hot jars and seal.

### Betty Snell's Rose and Rhubarb Syrup
(This is lovely over ice-cream.)

> 1 cup (250 ml) fragrant rose petals (dark are best)
> 1 lb. (500 g approximately) rhubarb
> 2 cups (500 ml) water
> 1½ cups (400 ml) sugar

Slice rhubarb and simmer till pulped. Strain, pour liquid back into saucepan, add sugar, rose petals (remove white heels) and stir well. Bring to boil and simmer 15 minutes, then strain. Bring syrup back to boil till deep red. Pour into warmed jars and seal.

### Rose Brandy

If you can bear to do this to a bottle of brandy, here is a recipe from a Virginia cookbook dated 1885. Gather petals from fragrant roses without bruising; fill a pitcher with them and cover with French brandy. Next day pour off the brandy, take out the petals, fill the pitcher with fresh ones and return the brandy. Do this until it is strongly impregnated, then bottle it.

Keep the pitcher loosely covered during the process. The brandy is good in cakes, fruit salads, puddings, ice creams, etc.

# Useful Addresses

The importation of live plants and plant materials across borders requires special arrangements, which will be detailed in suppliers' catalogs. Americans must have a permit, obtained through the Web site given below. Every order requires a phytosanitary certificate supplied by the exporter, and purchasers should verify this at the time of order. (If certain plants are exempt from this certificate, the seller will know.)

A CITES (Convention on International Trade in Endangered Species of Wild Fauna and Flora) certificate may also be required if the plant is an endangered species. For more information contact:
USDA-APHIS-PPQ
Permit Unit
4700 River Road, Unit 136
Riverdale, MD 20727-1236
Tel: (301) 734-8645. Fax: (301) 734-5786
www.aphis.usda.gov

Canadians importing plant material must pay a fee and complete an "application for permit to import." A phytosanitary certificate may also be required. For more information contact:
Plant Health and Production Division
Canadian Food Inspection Agency
2nd Floor West, Permit Office
59 Camelot Drive
Nepean, ON K1A 0Y9
Tel: (613) 225-2342. Fax: (613) 228-6605
www.inspection.gc.ca

The Heritage Roses Group is a fellowship of those who care about old roses. Members receive four issues of *Heritage Roses* annually. Membership covers U.S., Canada and Mexico. Contact:
Bev Dobson, Membership Secretary
916 Union Street, #302
Alameda, CA 94501

Many of the following nurseries will mail catalogs.

The Antique Rose Emporium
9300 Lueckemeyer Road
Brenham, TX 77833-6453
Tel: (979) 836-9051, for orders (800) 441-002
Fax: (979) 836-0928
*Roses are supplied on their own roots, i.e., they are not grafted onto other rootstock.*

B & B Nursery & Propagators
2578 Country Road 1
Willows, CA 95988
Tel/fax: (530) 934-2676
www.bandnursery.com
*Roses are supplied on their own roots, i.e., they are not grafted onto other rootstock.*

Chamblee's Rose Nursery
10926 U.S. Highway 69 North
Tyler, TX 75706-8742
Tel: (800) 256-7673. Fax: (903) 8882-3597
E-mail: roses@tyler.net
www.chambleeroses.com

David Austin Roses Ltd.
15059 Highway 64 West
Tyler, TX 75704
Tel: (903) 526-1800, (800) 328-8893
Fax: (903) 526-1900
E-mail:US@davidaustinroses.com

Freedom Gardens
6193 Vair Road
Freedom Twp, OH 44266
Tel: (330) 296-2618. Fax: (815) 364-1007
E-mail: FreedomGardens@cs.com

Heirloom Roses
20462 N.E. Riverside Drive
St. Paul, OR 97137
Tel: (505) 538-1576. Fax: (503) 538-5902
www.heirloomroses.com

Heritage Rosarium
211 Haviland Mill Road
Brookeville, MD 20833
Tel: (301) 774-6890
E-mail: Heritagero@aol.com

High Country Roses
Split Mountain Farm
9122 E. U.S. Highway 40
P.O. Box 148
Jensen, UT 84035
Tel: (435) 789-5512, (800) 552-2082
Fax: (435) 789-5517
E-mail: roses@easilink.com
www.highcountryroses.com

Hortico Inc.
723 Robson Road, R.R. 1
Waterdown, ON L0R 2H1
Tel: (905) 689-6984. Fax: (905) 689-6566
E-mail: office@hortico.com
www.hortico.com

Jackson & Perkins Co.
One Rose Lane
Medford, OR 97501
Tel: (877) 322-2300. Fax: (800) 242-0329
www.jacksonandperkins.com

Muncy's Rose Emporium
11207 Celestine Pass
Sarasota, FL 32240
Tel: (941) 377-6156
E-mail: ken@muncyrose.com
www.muncyrose.com

Old Heirloom Roses
P.O. Box 9106, Stn A
Halifax, NS B3K 5M7
Tel: (902) 471-3364
www.oldheirloomroses.com

Old Rose Nursery
Hornby Island, BC V0R 1Z0
Tel: (250) 335-2603
www.oldrosenursery.com

Pickering Nurseries
670 Kingston Road
Pickering, ON LIV 1A6
Tel: (905) 839-2111. Fax: (905) 839-4807
www.pickeringnurseries.com

Roses Unlimited
Route 1, Box 587
North Deerwood Drive
Laurens, SC 29360
Tel: (864) 682-7673. Fax: (864) 682-2455
E-mail: roseunlmt@aol.com
www.roseunlimitedownroot.com

Russian River Rose Company
1685 Magnolia Drive
Healdsburg, CA 95448
Tel: (707) 433-7455
www.Russian-River-Rose.com

Spring Valley Roses
N7637 – 330th Street
P.O. Box 7
Spring Valley, WI 54767
Tel: (715) 778-4481
E-mail:svroses@svtel.net
www.springvalleyroses.com

Vintage Gardens
2833 Old Gravenstein Highway South
Sebastopol, CA 95472
Tel: (707) 829-9516
www.vintagegardens.com

# Bibliography

Austin, David. *The Heritage of the Rose.*
   Suffolk: Antique Collectors' Club, 1986.
Austin, David. *Old Roses and English Roses.*
   Suffolk: Antique Collectors' Club, 1991.
Beales, Peter. *Classic Roses.*
   London: Collins Harvill, 1985.
Beales, Peter. *Twentieth Century Roses.*
   London: Collins Harvill, 1988.
Beales, Peter, et al. *Botanica's Roses.*
   Auckland: David Bateman Ltd., 1998.
Dickerson, Brent C. *The Old Rose Adventurer.*
   Portland: Timber Press, 1999.
Ellwanger, Henry B. *The Rose.*
   London: William Heinemann, 1893.
Fisher, John. *The Companion to Roses.*
   New York: Penguin Books Ltd., 1986.
Gibson, Michael. *The Book of the Rose.*
   London: Macdonald General Books, 1980.
Johnson, Hugh. *The Principles of Gardening.*
   London: Mitchell Beazley Publishers Ltd., 1979.
Pratt, Nigel. *Old Garden Roses in Summer.*
   Nelson: self-published, 1992.
Rohde, Eleanor Sinclair. *Rose Recipes from Olden
   Times.* New York: Dover Publications, 1973.
Ross, Deane M. *A Manual of Heritage Roses.*
   Adelaide: self-published, 1989.
Shoup, G. Michael. *Roses in the Southern Garden.*
   Brenham, Suffolk: The Antique Rose Emporium
   Inc., 2000.
Taylor, Barbara Lea. *Old-fashioned Roses.*
   Auckland: David Bateman Ltd., 1993.
Taylor, Barbara Lea. *David Austin's English Roses.*
   Auckland: David Bateman Ltd., 1994.

'Cottage Rose'

Taylor, Barbara Lea. *Growing Old-fashioned Roses.*
   Auckland: David Bateman Ltd., 1996.
Thomas, G. S. *The Old Shrub Roses.*
   London: J.M. Dent & Sons, 1955.
Journals of Heritage Rose Societies of America,
   Australia, England and New Zealand.

# Index

Numbers in bold indicate an illustration.

'A Shropshire Lad'  59, **59**
'Abraham'  58
'Abraham Darby'  58
'Adelaide d'Orléans'  28
'Agnes'  52, **52**
'Alba Maxima'  23
'Alba Semi-plena'  23, **23**
Albas  22–24
'Albéric Barbier'  29, **29**
'Alister Stella Gray'  35, 36
'Ambridge Rose'  59, **59**
'American Pillar'  29, **29**
'Anaïs Ségalas'  18, **18**
Apothecary's Rose  17
'Archduke Joseph'  **42**, 43
Austin, David  55–57
Austrian Copper  15
'Ballerina'  47, **47**
Banksia roses  13–14
Bare root roses  73–74
'Belle de Crécy'  18, **18**
'Belle des Jardins'  26
'Belle Poitevine'  53
'Belle Story'  59, **59**, **73**
'Blairii No. 2'  38, **38**
'Blanc Double de Coubert'  53, **53**
'Blue Rambler'  30
'Blythe Spirit'  59, **60**
Bourbon roses  37–40
'Brother Cadfael'  **58**, 60
'Buff Beauty'  48, **48**
'Cardinal de Richelieu'  18, **20**
'Cécile Brunner'  31, 32, **84**
'Céline Forestier'  36, **37**
'Centifolia Variegata'  26
Centifolias  24–26
'Chapeau de Napoléon'  27
'Charles de Mills'  19
'Charlotte'  60, **61**
Cherokee Rose  16
Cheshire Rose  23
Chestnut Rose  17
'Chianti'  60
China roses  31–34
'City of Portland'  45
Climbing roses  87–88
Climbing Tea roses  44–47
'Colonial White'  46

Companion plants  85–86
'Complicata'  **12**, 19, 21
'Comte de Chambord'  34, **34**
'Comte de Champagne'  **9**, 60
'Comtesse de Murinais'  27
'Comtesse du Cayla'  33
'Constance Spry'  56, 61, **57**
container-grown roses  74
containers, planting roses in  76
'Cornelia'  48, **48**, **72**
'Cottage Maid'  26
'Cottage Rose'  61, **94**
'Country Darby'  58
'Crépuscule'  36, **36**
'Crested Moss'  27
'Cristata'  27
'Crown Princess Margareta'  **8**, **60**, 61
'Cuisse de Nymphe'  24
Cuttings  77–78
'Dainty Bess'  44, **44**
Damasks  21–22
'Dapple Dawn'  61
Deadheading  77
'Desprez à Fleur Jaune'  36
'Devoniensis'  45, **45**
Diseases  83
  black spot  **82**, 83
  powdery mildew  83, **83**
  rust  83
  Dog Rose  23
'Duc de Cambridge'  22
'Duchesse de Brabant'  43, **43**
'Duchesse d'Istrie'  28
'Duchesse de Montebello'  19, **19**
Early hybrid tea roses  42–44
'Eglantyne'  61, **61**
'Eglantyne Jebb'  61
'Evelyn'  62, **62**
'Ever-blooming Dr. Van Fleet'  50
'Fair Bianca'  62
Fall Damask  21
'Falstaff'  62, **62**
'Fantin Latour'  **25**, 26
Feeding roses  76–77
'Félicité Parmentier'  23
'Ferdinand Pichard'  41
Four Seasons Rose  21
Fragrance  85
'François Juranville'  30, **30**
'Frau Dagmar Hastrup'  53, **53**
Gallicas  17–21
'Gardenia'  30, **30**

'Général Galliéni'  44, **44**
'Général Lamarque'  36
'Gertrude Jekyll'  62
'Ghislaine de Féligonde'  49, **49**
'Glamis Castle'  63
'Gloire de Dijon'  45, **45**, **88**
'Golden Celebration'  **62**, 63
'Golden Rambler'  35
'Grace'  **55**, 63
'Graham Thomas'  63, **63**
Great Double White  23
Groundcovers, roses as  88
'Gruss an Aachen'  50, **50**
'Gruss an Teplitz'  **32**, 33
'Hansa'  53
'Happy Child'  63
Hardiness Zone Map  **7**
Hedges, roses as  88
'Henri Martin'  27, **27**
'Heritage'  63
Himalayan Musk Rose  14
'Hippolyte'  **19**, 20
'Honorine de Brabant'  **38**, 39
'Hume's Blush'  31
Hybrid Musk roses  47–49
Hybrid perpetuals  40–42
Hybrid Tea roses  44–47
'Incarnata'  24
'Ispahan'  22, **22**
Jacobite Rose  23
'Jacquenetta'  64
'Jacques Cartier'  34, **34**
'Jaune Desprez'  36
'Jean Ducher'  43, **43**
'John Clare'  64, **64**
'Kathryn Morley'  64, **64**
'Königin von Dänemark'  **23**, 24
'L.D. Braithwaite'  64, **65**
'La Royale'  24
'La Rubanée'  26
'La Séduisante'  24
'Lady Hillingdon'  45
'Lamarque'  36, **37**, **49**
'Laure Davoust'  30,
'Leander'  65, **65**
'Leda'  22, **22**
'Louise Odier'  39, **39**
'Lucetta'  65
'Magnolia Rose'  45
'Maiden's Blush'  24
'Marchesa/Marquise Boccella'  34, **34**
'Mary Rose'  65, **80**

'May Queen' 50, **50**
'Mermaid' 50
'Miss Alice' 65
'Mlle de Sombreuil' 46
'Mme. Alfred Carrière' **1**, 37
'Mme. Caroline Testout' 45
'Mme. Hardy' **21**, 22
'Mme. Isaac Pereire' 39, **39**
'Mme. Lauriol de Barny' **11**, 39
'Mme. Legras de St. Germain' 24
'Mme. Louis Levêque' 27, **28**
'Mme. Plantier' 24, **24**
'Molyneux' 66, **66**
'Moonlight' 48, **49**
'Morning Mist' 66, **66**
Moss roses 26–28
'Mrs. John Laing' 41, **41**
Mulching 77
'Mutabilis' **32**, 33
'New Dawn' 50
Noisette roses 35–37
'Old Blush' 31, 33, **33**
'Old Pink Monthly' 33
'Old Velvet Moss' 28
'Park's Yellow' 31
'Parson's Pink China' 31, 33
'Pat Austin' 67
'Paul Ricault' 41, **41**
'Paul Transon' 51, **51**
'Penelope' **11**, 48, **49**
'Perle d'Or' 34
Pests 81–83
  aphids 82, **82**
  caterpillars 82
  curculio weevils 83
  Japanese beetles 83
  red spider mites 82
  spraying 81
  white scale 82
'Petite de Hollande' 26
'Phyllis Bide' 51
Planting 74–76
  bare root roses 74, 75
  climbers 75
  container-grown roses 74, 75
  standard roses 76
Portland roses 34–35
'Pretty Jessica' 67, **67**

Propagation 77–78
  container method 78
  open ground 78
Protection from cold 78–79
Pruning 79–81
  climbers 80
  English roses 80
  hedges 80
  old roses 80
  once-flowering roses 79
  ramblers 80–81
  repeat-flowering roses 79
  standards 81
'Queen of Denmark' 24
'Queen of the Violets' 42
Ramblers 28–30, 49–51
'Red Coat' 67, **67**
'Reine des Violettes' 42, **42**
*Rosa alba* 23
*Rosa banksiae lutea* 14, **14**
*Rosa brunonii* 14, **14**
*Rosa canina* 23
*Rosa chinensis* 31
*Rosa damascena* 23
*Rosa damascena bifera* 21
*Rosa dupontii* 14, **15**, **75**
*Rosa eglanteria* 15, **15**
*Rosa foetida bicolor* 15, **16**
*Rosa gallica* 17
*Rosa gallica officinalis* 17
*Rosa gallica versicolor* 20
*Rosa glauca* **15**, 16
*Rosa laevigata* 16, **16**
*Rosa moyesii* 16, **16**
*Rosa mulliganii* 17
'Rosa Mundi' 20, **20**
*Rosa rugosa* Alba 52, **52**
*Rosa roxburghii plena* 17
Rose à Quatre Saisons 21
'Rose de Rescht' 35, **35**
Rose forms **10**
Rose oil 90
Rose recipes 90–91
'Roseraie de l'Hay' 54, **54**
Rugosa roses 51–54
'Safrano' 44
'Salut d'Aix la Chapelle' 50
'Sharifa Asma' 67

'Shropshire Lass' 67
Shrub-climbers 49–51
Shrub roses 49–51, 86–87
  pegging down 87
'Slater's Crimson China' 31
'Sombreuil' 46, **46**
'Souvenir de la Malmaison' 40, **40**
'Souvenir de Mme. Léonie Viennot'
  **46**, 47
'Souvenir de Philemon Cochet' 54, **54**
'Souvenir de St Anne's' 40, **40**
Spraying 81
Standard roses 87
'Stanwell Perpetual' **50**, 51
'Sweetheart Rose' 32
'Sweet Briar' 15
'Sweet Juliet' 68, **69**
Tea roses 42–44
'Teasing Georgia' 68, **69**
'The Countryman' 68
'The Dark Lady' 68, **69**
'The Herbalist' 68, **69**
'The Maréchal' 36
'The Mayflower' 68, 69
'The Pilgrim' 69
'The Prince' 70
'Tipo Ideale' 33
'Tour de Malakoff' 26, **26**
Transplanting 76
'Vanity' 49
'Veilchenblau' 30
'Victoria' 45
'Village Maid' **25**, 26
'Violet Blue' 30
'Virginale' 24
'Virginia R. Coxe' 33
Watering roses 77
'Wenlock' 70, **70**
White Rose of York 23
'William Lobb' 28, **28**
'William Morris' **2**, 56, 70
'William Shakespeare 2000' **57**, 70
'Winchester Cathedral' 70, **70**
'Windrush' 70, **71**
'Yellow Banksia' 14
'Yellow Cécile Brunner' 34
'Zephirine Drouhin' **6**, 40

## Picture credits

The following photographs have been supplied by DAVID AUSTIN – p. 2 'William Morris' (Auswill);
p. 8 'Crown Princess Margareta' (Auswinter); p. 55 and back cover 'Grace' (Auskeppy); p. 56 'William Morris' (Auswill);
p. 57 'William Shakespeare 2000' (Ausromeo); p. 60 'Blythe Spirit' (Auschool); 'Crown Princess Margareta' (Auswinter);
p. 62 'Falstaff' (Ausverse); p. 68 'The Mayflower' (Austilly); p. 69 'Teasing Georgia' (Ausbaker)
BARBARA LEA TAYLOR – p. 6 'Zepherine Drouhin'; p. 11 'Mme. Lauriol de Barny'; p. 18 'Belle de Crécy'; p. 42 'Reine des
Violettes'; p. 49 'Penelope'; p. 57 'Constance Spry'; p. 67 'Pretty Jessica'; p. 69 'The Herbalist'; p. 70 'Winchester Cathedral';
p. 75 *Rosa dupontii*